Dedication

I would like to dedicate this book to My Lord and Savior Jesus Christ.

- For healing my mind, body, soul, and spirit

- For the experience of going through to get to my blessings.

- To my husband and children for walking with me "Against All Odds".

Acknowledgements

First of all, I would like to give a Special thanks to Our Lord and Savior Jesus Christ for life, health, and strength to write this book. Thank you for choosing me to be used for your glory. Thank you for saving me, delivering me, and healing me. I really Love You Lord.

- I would like to give special thanks to my husband for your love, support, prayers and always being there. 35 years and counting! So grateful for you my Mighty Man of Valor. I love you always and forever.

- To my children Jennifer, Derrick Jr., and Jasmine; my Three Musketeers (God's Infantry Soldiers), thank you for loving me, supporting me and being the best children a mother could ever pray for. It is an honor to be your mother. I love you with all my heart always and forever.

-To my sons-in-love George and Marcus, what a blessing you are. Thank you for your love and loving our daughters the way Christ loves the church.

- To my grand-blessings, Destiny, Miracle, Daniel, and Mariah Jai; you all are the daily smile in my heart. I am a blessed and happy Nana. You all bring me so much joy. Love you little grands always and forever.

- To my mother-in-love Janeen Stewart, thank you for your love, support, and prayer. I love you and you are a blessing from the father above.

-To my sisters-in-love Minister Shaya and Evangelist Sabrina, thank you for taking good care of me. Your love and support over the years has been priceless. Love you.

-To my sister Cheri Travis, I love you with all of my heart, and I praise God that we found each other after 30 years.

-To Tonika, my spiritual daughter, thank you for helping me accomplish my goal in finishing my book. You are such a blessing and a gift from God.

-To The Faith Church Family, you all are the best! Thank you for your faithfulness, love, support, encouraging spirit and your dedication and diligence to the work of the Lord. I am a blessed Pastor. You have helped me to grow in the Lord in so many ways. Words can not express my gratitude and the love I have in my heart for all of you.

- To my spiritual parents Pastor's Bob and Martha Ruth Kirkley, thank you for seeing the call of God on my life and helping mature the gifts in me. Thank you for your prayers, for fighting for my soul, for standing with me in sunshine and rain, sickness and pain. You two are gifts from God. I am forever grateful and so blessed to be your daughter. I love you.

- To The Beeler Family and The Smith Family, I love you all from the bottom of my heart.

A special thanks to all the individuals, churches, family and friends that prayed for me and are still praying for me. I am forever grateful to you all. Love and Blessings to you until He returns.

Apostle Jeff and Jane Johns

Pastor's Bob and Martha Ruth Kirkley

Bishop Leonard and First Lady Christine Scott

Pastor's Bryant and Ta'Sha Scott

Pastor Shirley Caesar

Evangelist Carolyn Sanders

Pastor John P. Kee and First Lady Felice Kee

New Life Community Choir

Pastor's Walter and Elaine Walters

Pastor's Eddie and Notoshia Howard

Pastor Tonya Burris-Mallory

Bishop D.K. and Pastor Alice Jones

Pastor Donald and First Lady Yvonne Tucker

Pastor Ronald and Sister Cathy Tucker

Pastor Kevin Russell

Minister Angela Rowe

Minister Ellen Russell Churchwell

Pastor Marvin Dale Churchwell

Pastor Steven and Sister Karen Russell

Pastor Pamela Horne

Pastor Arthur and First Lady McClendon

Pastors James and Pamela Harlan

Pastor Johnson Beaven

Elder Kaloma and Prophetess Takeya Davis

Elder Keith McGaw

Darryl and Vivian Barner

Betty Allen

Gail Russell Freeman

Gloria Williams

Sharena Lynem

Mother Barbara Coleman

Minister Gerald Jones

Cynthia Roper

Tammy Malone

Janice Prince

Paula Sargeant

Portia Jackson

Deborah Sargent

Tony Harvey

Tracy Wilder

Tina Hardiman

James Hewlett

Connie Sykes

Milika Rush

Kimberly Reed

TaMara Goode

Pamela and Darryl White & Family

Special Thanks to Breakthrough Ministries
www.intercessors.org
breakthrough@intercessors.org
Thank you for your intercession over the years

Foreword

By Bishop Leonard S. Scott, DDS

And they overcame him by the blood of the Lamb, and by the word of their testimony; and they loved not their lives unto the death. Revelation 12:11

The Christian's personal testimony is extremely powerful. Many of us fail to realize or understand the awesome weapon in spiritual warfare that we possess in our testimony. Often we may fail to speak up for the cause of Christ because we feel like we do not have sufficient theological knowledge to make our case. The truth is no amount of human cogitation can negate the facts of the miracles God has performed in your life. The Pharisees spent an inordinate amount of time trying to invalidate the ministry of Jesus using the theological thoughts of their culture. But their intellectual opinions could not nullify the testimony of the blind man seeing, of the lame man walking, the dumb man talking, the deaf man hearing and Lazarus being brought back to life after four days in the grave.

I first met Pastor Denise Carpenter as a result of appearing on a local Trinity Broadcasting Network television program. I was promoting a music project we were planning that would include singers from all over the Indianapolis Metropolitan area who loved to praise the Lord. As a result Denise contacted us with interest in participating on the project. Our meeting was the beginning of a lasting relationship and fruitful friendship.

Denise became an instrumental member in that musical and singing aggregation, the Garment of Praise, participating in three nationally distributed Praise and Worship projects from the group. Because of her exemplary markcting and promotions skills she was hired by Tyscot Records to promote the various artists on our roster. She went on to form her own Gospel youth group known as the Jesus Gang, who would travel all over the nation proclaiming the gospel of Jesus Christ in song and word.

Later the Lord called Denise and her husband Reverend Derrick Carpenter to start a church. They birthed a ministry in inner city Indianapolis that has resulted in the lives of many being reached and changed for Christ. They continue to this day to impact that community with the gospel through the church and various other outreach efforts. During the course of these events, Pastor Denise was attacked in her body by the adversary. So many people are living under tremendous pressures of life and breaking under the strains of contemporary culture. This book shares Pastor Denise Carpenter's unique testimony and tells her exciting and encouraging story of how faith in God brought her out against all odds.

Bishop Leonard Scott, DDS
Pastor Rock Community Church & Tyscot Music, Film + Entertainment, Founder.

Preface

Odds are defined as unusual, rare, and uncommon. Odds are also described as an advantage, or favoring one side of two opposing parties. These two definitions together create the story of my life. One where the road wasn't always known, and the trials, temptations, and tribulations weren't expected; but with God's favor on my side I have been victorious in this Christian walk. Coming from a single-parent family, losing my father at an early age, my mother and brother-in-law passing in their sleep, becoming extremely ill unto death, not obeying God to preach the Gospel, my husband losing his job, losing our home to foreclosure, our oldest daughter getting pregnant out of wedlock, to losing our second-born granddaughter, all of this in a very short amount of time; I have learned that you have to go through to get to, so that you can rise as a conqueror "Against all Odds." A true testimony doesn't begin until you experience the odds against you. This is my story of conquering the odds against me, and I am blessed to share it with you.

TABLE OF CONTENTS

From Problems to Promotion

From Overload to Overcoming

Against All Odds Healing Scriptures

Contact Information:
Pastor Lauren Denise Carpenter
Church Website: www.thefaithchurchministries.com
Facebook: www.facebook.com/LDeniseCarpenter
Twitter: www.twitter/com/PastorDenise7
Email: AAObook1@gmail.com

Book Cover Design: Derrick S. Carpenter Jr.

Book Editor: Jasmine Carpenter- Elliott & TaMara E. Goode

*All Reference Scriptures are from King James and New King James Versions

Chapter One

WHY DO BAD THINGS HAPPEN TO GOOD PEOPLE?

<u>From Sorrow to Songs</u>

For me, music carries with it not only rhythm and sound but elicits some of the most pleasant memories I have. With a musical background on both my parent's side, I grew up listening to a range of music as a little girl. Artists such as Aretha Franklin, Smokey Robinson, The Temptations, and Michael Jackson, were just a few. Music has always been a part of me, and so it is not unusual that it was one of the main motivational tools that carried me throughout the most difficult times in my life.

In 1998, my life was dealt two devastating blows; the sudden loss of my mother and an unknown illness that threatened my life. At the age of 36, when my mother passed away suddenly in her sleep, I was both grief-stricken and bitter about her passing. I could not understand the question that had been lingering in my

mind for so long. *Why do bad things happen to good people?* I

didn't realize that later that same year another major life event

would happen that would result in me asking that same question

again.

It seemed as if out of nowhere, I was suddenly struck with

an illness in my body that the doctors, still to this day, have no

explanation for. My symptoms included epileptic seizures, organ

failure, an extremely high blood pressure of 218/190, losing the use

of all my limbs, and being paralyzed with chronic pain. The

doctors presented several diagnoses ranging from AIDS, cancer,

lupus, rheumatoid arthritis, and many more ailments. The sad and

discouraging news was that they had no idea what was going on. I

was taking over twenty-two medications, enduring chemo-therapy

treatments weekly, losing my hair, undergoing dialysis and

breaking out with abrasions all over my body. The pictures that I

selected to share throughout the book are evidence of my

experience and testimony being true.

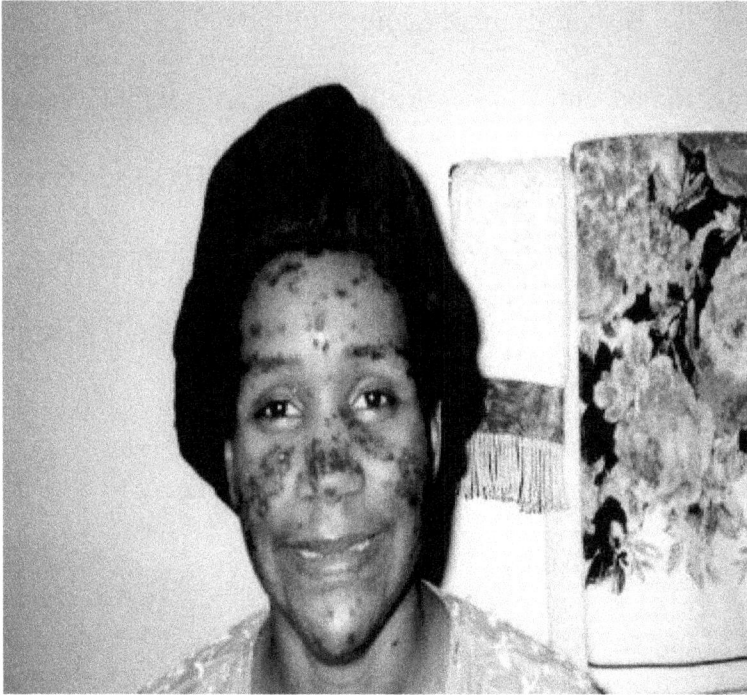

Looking at the above picture, you can see how the odds were definitely against me, but God was for me. The Lord provided me with the strength to make it, and a lot of that strength came from listening and being inspired by the music that is so much a part of me today. Songs such as, "I Really Love the Lord" by Rev. Charles Nicks Jr., "I Feel Like Going On" by Keith Pringle, "There is No Way" by Rev. Milton Brunson, "Total Praise" by Richard Smallwood, "He's Working it Out" by Pastor Shirley Caesar, "Only

Believe" by Bishop Leonard Scott, "Still I Rise" by Yolanda Adams, and the entire *Strength* album, by Pastor John P. Kee and New Life, really helped me during my illness. These songs touched my body, spirit, and soul and if I were to choose a theme song during my illness, it would be "Still I Rise" by Yolanda Adams from her CD, *Songs from the Heart*. The lyrics that still ring dear in my heart say, "Yet still I rise, never to give up, never to give in, against all odds." This is the song that inspired the title of this book. I learned to turn my sorrow into songs. Psalm 32:7, *Thou art my hiding place, thou shalt preserve me from trouble; thou shalt compass me about with songs of deliverance.*

From Depression to Discipline

Even with all the lovely music pounding into my heart along with my prayers, and reading of the Word, I still battled with a depression. *Why?* I asked myself and still I could not understand why these things were happening to me. Granted, I had made some mistakes earlier in my life when my boyfriend and I were not married but were sexually active with each other. Ultimately, the sin of fornication finally caught up with us and during this time frame, I had gotten pregnant twice and aborted them both. I was not perfect, but after the abortions I had decided to do things the right way. My boyfriend, who was also my high school sweetheart, married me and is now my loving husband with whom I have three beautiful children; Jennifer, Derrick Jr., and Jasmine. My family has always been active in ministry and working with inner-city youth in turning their lives away from delinquent and illicit behavior towards God. We started a city wide youth choir called the "Jesus Gang", and they became national recording artist on Tyscot Records Label. The Jesus Gang traveled across the country inspiring young people to live for Jesus in a language the youth could relate to.

Another vision from God that we had also received a word and confirmation on was to develop The Ark of Safety, a youth center that would focus on redirecting young lives from the streets to Jesus. We did the best we could to make the scripture come alive: *as for me and my house, we will serve the Lord.* However, I could not fathom why God would allow these things to happen to such a dedicated and committed family, but He did. I had buried my mother, and soon feared that my children would be burying me. In addition to the twenty-two medications, chemo-therapy, losing my hair, breaking out in abrasions, and being placed on dialysis, I faced new challenges as my kidneys began to fail and my heartbeat became irregular. The doctors didn't know what else to do so they experimented and gave me more medications to take. It was not long after that I was admitted to the hospital, one of three hospital stays, which is where the story of facing the odds against me really begins.

From Bitter to Better

When my mother died, I was naturally sad and eventually became bitter. My bitterness reached a deeper level because it was combined with the feeling of being incomplete. The main reason for this feeling that I was experiencing was due to an unfulfilled and unsupported call on my life. I belonged to a very traditional Baptist Church from the age of ten years old. I had a wonderful Pastor and First Lady who were great spiritual parents, but our pastor did not believe in women preachers being licensed. They were still a tremendous blessing to us and provided me with a very strong foundation in the Lord. They taught my husband and me valuable lessons about serving the Lord that we both cherish to this day. We loved and highly respected both of our spiritual parents. Nevertheless, tradition in the Baptist Church at that time did not allow a woman to be licensed to preach. Although I was very active in the church as a missionary, youth teacher, youth director, and choir director, I certainly was not a preacher or pastor. I was faced with a spiritual confliction as I knew I was being called to preach because God had spoken to me in a dream and confirmed this calling on my life many times.

However, when I took it to my Pastor he would say, "You have to have something to preach about. Where's your testimony?"

In other words, at twenty years old, I didn't have very much of a testimony at that time. I will never forget those words that he spoke, but I would still ask him quite often if he would license me to preach, and he would say "No". Eventually, like many other women who were called to do what was then deemed as only "male" roles in some Baptist churches, I felt frustrated and incomplete. Although I could never understand this glass ceiling in the foundation of some churches, I knew all too well from firsthand experience that it did exist. The only person that I would confide in about this issue that was bothering me so much was my mother, who had now been taken from me when I needed her the most. The loss of my mom, coupled with the unfulfilled call on my life, filled me with bitterness and grief.

My body began to ache all over, but I continued to ignore it, believing the pain would eventually go away. Yet, the pain persisted and even began to get progressively worse. Finally, the pain had gotten so unbearable that I decided to go get a checkup, and this time the doctors diagnosed me with rheumatoid arthritis and gave me medication to take for it that failed to work. The only thing that brought me any type of relief was going to my prayer closet. It is during this time that I fell in love with intercessory prayer, and even though I prayed fervently I still continued to take the medications the doctors prescribed that was not working. No one, including the doctors, could understand why. Whenever the doctors noted that the medications failed to work, they would then change my diagnosis, this time telling me that I may have the AIDS virus. Now this was a diagnosis that I knew to be impossible as I had only been with one man my entire life, Derrick, my high school sweetheart and husband. We had been married for sixteen years and were together for twenty-one years, with neither of us having used intravenous drugs nor had been unfaithful. We knew AIDS was a lie from the pits of hell, and there was no way I was going to accept or claim that diagnosis.

From Discombobulation to Determination

Eventually, the medications the doctors gave me began to change things in my body, and unfortunately it was not the change for the better that we were looking forward to. The various medicines were having an adverse effect, resulting in psychotic and emotional episodes. I was becoming increasingly depressed, unable to think clearly, and did not feel totally like myself. I was feeling extremely "off", and my behavior began to reflect this. Even though my mind and body wasn't operating at 100%, I remained in tune spiritually, and because of this I had a precognitive notion that the doctors were going to send some people to my house to take me away and commit me to the hospital psychiatric ward. I clearly saw the police lights and heard the sirens in my vision, and I had decided that before any of this could happen I needed to get away. When I did try to tell people, they thought I was just hallucinating and being paranoid because they could not believe God was actually showing me what was soon to happen.

One day, I decided I would leave the house so that no one would be able to come get me. The medications had such an effect on me that I could not think my plan out carefully, but I knew I had to leave. I first went next door and started making phone calls for someone to pick me up. Finally, my friend Pastor Tonya came over to the house upon my request that she take me to the store to pick up some things. I desperately tried explaining what was going on to her, but she could not understand any of it, and I realize now that most people back then wouldn't have been able to comprehend my plight either. Nonetheless, I was frustrated because I needed help and couldn't seem to get it. Overwhelmed, I got out of the car and started walking away down the street. Meanwhile back home, my children were able to reach a cousin of mine named Tony to help come find me. When Tony found me, he picked me up and took me to see one of his friends, a nurse at Med- Check. The nurse then informed me I needed to go to the hospital, and of course I refused to go because I was afraid they would commit me to the psychiatric ward like the one I had seen in my precognitive notion. When I came home, the children had called their dad and told him what was going on and that I was acting strange. My husband called the doctor, who told me to come in immediately and again, I said no. In addition to the visions I had seen, I was also tired of going back and forth to the doctor. We sent the children with my sister-in-law Shaya for the rest of the day until we could make up our minds about what to do. After the children left, my husband came upstairs and laid his hands on me in prayer. I was really sick, and he knew there was nothing else to do if I refused to go to the hospital. Derrick was on his knees praying for me while I was in the bed, when out of nowhere I began to hear police sirens and see the police lights. Upon realizing that they weren't there, I asked Derrick if he heard or noticed what I had seen, but he had not. It was only just moments later that the visions I had tried to tell people about had finally manifested. Followed by an ambulance, the police arrived at our residence and gained entrance to our home through our garage door. They had a court order seeking to arrest my husband for neglecting to take me to the hospital. It also gave them the authority to take me to the hospital, because if they didn't detain me, I would die. I was hysterical! I screamed and demanded that they not take my husband to jail, informing them that I told my husband that I did not want to go to the hospital, because if God didn't heal me as He said in His Word, then I didn't want to be here anymore. The police officers decided it was in my best interest not to arrest my husband, allowing him to stay with me. However, there was no negotiating on whether I would go to the hospital or not, so I was placed in the ambulance and taken directly there. Yes, it was true that I had been seeing things, but I was definitely not hallucinating! Though I was not committed to a psychiatric ward as I had feared, I was in the hospital and this is where the story of my first three hospital stays began.

Blizzard of 1998-1999: From Betrayal to Boldness

It was during my hospitalization in January of 1999 that Indianapolis experienced an extreme blizzard, which resulted in the city being shut down and no one was able to get in or out of the hospital. My husband and I were stuck in the hospital together with God for two weeks, and while we were there the doctors, upon my insistence, conducted another AIDS test on me which returned back negative. The doctors had obviously made a mistake and were convinced that if it wasn't the AIDS virus, that it had to be something else. Soon after, I was then diagnosed with lupus, which the doctors were still unsure about. For several years, I was like their personal guinea pig as they tried to fix me with no solutions, but I was also equipped with a strong Spirit of God that refused to just take what the devil tried to serve me.

From Trouble to Trust

My body was in trouble, but my spirit was trusting in God's word. The rough days and nights at the hospital fighting for my life felt like an eternity to me. All I could think about was how unfair this situation was to my family and everyone else who loved and depended on us. I tried to stay positive, and instead of putting all my focus on the trouble, I put more of my trust in God. I read my

Word daily from a Bible I kept with me all the time called my "Blue Bible" because it's blue, and I still have it to this day. This Bible is over 25 years old, and I would not let my Bible leave my side or let anyone take it from me. While in the hospital, I held on to my Bible for dear life because it was my life source, and I knew it. I would put dates next to everything I read and would highlight all the scriptures I felt God was speaking to me. My whole bible is marked up from me writing in it from Genesis to Revelation. The things I wrote in it are so priceless to me. My "Blue Bible" still confirms things from God to this day.

Along with reading the Word, I made sure to fill my atmosphere with praise and worship. I repeatedly listened to the song "I'm Healed in Jesus Name," by Pastor John P. Kee along with healing scriptures on cassette tapes. I know that through this song and others, God was indeed providing my entire being with strength and healing. The book of Psalms is my favorite; there are two scriptures I recall to remembrance that really supported how I felt at that time. Psalm 77:6 - *I call to remembrance my song in the night.* I did exactly that, with yet another Psalm 42:8 - *Yet the Lord will command His loving kindness in the day time, and in the night His song shall be with me, and my prayer unto the God of my life.* I thank God for His Word and the songs of deliverance that He gave me.

From Enemies to Endurance

One day, while attending a church; still believing in God for my total healing, a Prophet of the Lord came to me. The prophet said, "God said, the only thing you have is an iron deficiency. The medicines you're taking are making you sicker." This was confirmation.

I believed in this word because I was definitely not feeling any better and in all actuality, I was getting worse. This was ironic because when I began to heal, and after taking all other types of medication, I was then given iron pills to take daily and B12 shots to shoot in my leg for energy. I believe if I had been given that same prescription when my sickness first began, I might not have been as sick as I was. Nevertheless, God had made my body strong, so I was able to withstand all the different medications the doctors had given me. For years, I sang a song in church entitled "Better Lord", and to my surprise the lyrics literally became my personal testimony. The song said, "If it takes all the worldly things from my life, make me better Lord. And if it means that I have a lot to sacrifice, make me better Lord. Even if it means sometimes, I have to fight with tear stained eyes, make me better Lord. Even if it means sometimes I falter when I try; I'll get up and go on, if it makes me strong; because I want to give you my best, and I'll only be hurting myself, if I tried to give you less. And if it means sometimes, the road will get rough, make me better Lord. I'll go on, just knowing, that your grace will be enough, to make me better Lord. I want to be better than good enough; cause just being good won't be quite enough. Lord make me ready, to stand my test. I want to be ready to do my best. Make me better."

I sang this song from the bottom of my heart. My life has been tested and tried by each word that the song portrays, but I thank God that He sustained me. As in Hebrews 5:8 - *Though he were a Son, yet learned He obedience by the things which He suffered.* I've learned obedience through all my sufferings.

I have to pause and take a PRAISE Break. Thank You Lord for healing me! I'm healed in Jesus Name; no more sickness, no more pain. By His stripes we shall all proclaim, I'm healed in Jesus Name. Hallelujah!

Chapter Two

SIGNS THAT GOD WAS WITH ME

From Conflict to Compassion

During my time in the hospital, I did not lose sight of the calling on my life to preach, and I set out to do just that after I was released. In order to live out the call on my life as a minister and preacher of the Gospel, my family and I left our previous church and went to St. Paul AME. Pastor Walters, Rev. Elaine Walters and the entire St. Paul AME Church covered us with love and prayer. On Sunday, May 16, 1999, I was finally given the honor of preaching my first initial sermon. It was titled, "A Blessing in Disguise", and was based off the scripture 1 Peter 4:12-13, *Beloved think it not strange concerning the fiery trial which is to try you, as though some strange thing happened unto you. But rejoice in as much as ye are partakers of Christ's sufferings; that, when his glory shall be revealed, ye may be glad also with exceeding joy.* The reason behind this title can be seen in what I was going though at the time and what would later become the strongest testimony I have; the fight for my life. People, even believers, think there is something wrong if you are suffering, but God tells us in the scripture that it is not unusual for the children of Christ to suffer. Look at the story of Job. I have often been told that my testimony parallels the story of Job. His friends thought he had sin in his life because of all the trouble that suddenly came upon him. I am sure people thought the same about me. I was even told by some to repent because I must have a secret sin somewhere in my closet, since I was having so much trouble in my life at the time. Job's wife told him to curse God and die, and because he was so sick and had lost everything he owned, she had lost faith in God. I thank God my husband was encouraging, faithful, and steadfast; not having the mindset to lose faith in God. He was always praying and believing for my healing and trusting God even when he could not trace God. It is so important to marry the person God has chosen for you because you will live out your vows for better or for worse, for richer or poorer in sickness and in health. If I had married the wrong man I would be dead today. I thank the Lord for my husband daily and for standing in faith with God for my life. My husband and I learned that since we are both shareholders and partakers of the crown, we are to suffer as Christ did, just as we will reign as He did. This was more than enough reason to be joyful, even in times of great suffering, like when our life is the thing at stake. This message comforted me and I'm sure many others who were experiencing some type of suffering. It showed God will always be with us in the midst of our trials. We must take courage in times of crisis.

After being at St. Paul AME for a while, we attended and later joined a church called Immanuel House of Prayer. This church was known for PRAYING people through the types of situations that I was experiencing at the time. Bishop D.K., Pastor Alice Jones and the congregation at the church stood by our side and supported us through my sickness, which would become a three year ordeal. This church also holds special significance for me because this is where we met our spiritual parents, Pastor's Bob and Martha Ruth Kirkley. The Kirkleys were a tremendous blessing to my family and I, and they directed us into the will of God for our lives. I will discuss them a lot more in detail later in the book because they were a huge sign that God was with us. Though I didn't know it at the time, I would undergo two more hospital stays before I would be able to begin walking in my complete healing.

From Hell to Heaven

The rest of the year 1999 went pass without any more incidents as it relates to my health. Then in 2000, I was rushed to the E.R. with a massive headache, blurred vision, and seeing only a mirage of colors. It had gotten so bad that while on route to the hospital, I literally went blind! Once at the hospital, the doctors prepared me for an x-ray, fearing that the cause of the headaches could potentially be due to my brain swelling. As I laid on a gurney in the corner awaiting x-rays, a "couple of minutes" waiting turned into a half hour of me fighting off seizures. I thought I was going to die because the fight was making me weaker and weaker. But,

God's word says He will never put more on us than we can bear. Finally, when it came to the point that I could no longer control the seizures, God gave me a sign that said He was definitely with me.

A stranger, who I believe to this day to have been an angel sent by God, came out of nowhere and said, "This lady needs help. She is going into a seizure."

The doctors later informed me that my brain was swollen, and I was immediately admitted to the hospital for two weeks. Hebrews 13:2 - Be *not forgetful to entertain strangers: for thereby some have entertained angels unawares.* Over the course of my sickness, I had many experiences of divine intervention that literally saved my life. I have no doubt that they were angels on assignment watching over me.

My final hospital stay came in 2001. It is the longest, most memorable, and intense stay out of the three that I had experience. I was in the hospital for forty days, and during those forty days, I fell into a coma. Often, you hear about people going into comas, not remembering anything that occurred, and sometimes waking up not even knowing who they are. My coma was not like this. I believe God allowed this because He wanted me to be able to recall the best thing that had ever happened to me; my out of body experience with God. I know there are many people who have had experiences such as I had, going to Heaven and returning to tell their story like I did. I believe, as they may believe also, that my proof rests in my healing and the life that God allowed me to continue to live so that I can share this story with you.

When I fell into my coma, the first thing I remember is my walk with Jesus on the sea shore and in the green valley. In the valley the grass was so green and beautiful. It was a green I had never seen, so vibrant and full of life. I saw beautiful cows with black and white colors that were just breath taking. It was ironic that I thought they were so beautiful because on earth, I saw cows as the ugliest animal. But in Heaven, everything is beautiful! There are no words to describe the water off of the sea shores in Heaven. I've seen the Hawaii shores and they are beautiful, but Hawaii waters are no comparison to Heaven's shores. I just kept staring at it all in total amazement. The most memorable encounter I had while in Heaven was feeling the love of God and it was the greatest love of all. I felt so fulfilled and whole in His love, which was all around me wherever I turned. I did not want to leave such peace, beauty, and love; I wanted to stay there forever. So when Jesus told me I had to go back to this world, I broke out in tears.

I tried saying everything I could in order to stay, but He said, "I know you want to stay here and that you are tired of being in pain, but you will be fine. You have to go back for your children and all the other children and people I have called you to. I have more work for you to do. I have chosen you and placed you on a special assignment that I will assign to you in your future. There are some souls that will only be saved, healed, and delivered by hearing the words I will speak through you."

I could not believe He wanted me to leave Him and this beautiful paradise to go back to a world filled with darkness, violence, and hate. I did not understand, and I tried to negotiate with Jesus. I told Him that what I am seeing from up here in Heaven, the children would be fine, including mine. He had plenty of people on earth who He could speak through to spread the gospel, but He had a different plan. He had chosen me, and nothing I could say would ever change that. As I think about that experience of me trying to negotiate with Him, like I had negotiating power to change His will for my life, I still chuckle because He really took the time to listen to all my reasons why I should stay with Him in Heaven. He could have just said "No" and "Go", but He was so kind, loving, caring, and patient. I did not want to return then, but as I reflect on it now, I am glad that I stopped negotiating and just trusted and obeyed Him. It is a lesson we must all learn. Just obey; God's way is better than ours.

The last thing I remember is Jesus telling me He loved me and to not be afraid to go back because He was with me, and He would make me strong in the Lord. I believe He allowed me to experience Heaven to show me what my reward would be for my obedience and suffering, and also so I would not lose heart and give up. Proverbs 13:12 - *Hope deferred maketh the heart sick; but when the desire cometh, it is a tree of life.* Let me be the first to admit that though I was not very optimistic then, I know now that whatever we go through in this life is worth it because of the reward we shall receive later. 1 Corinthians 2:9 - *But as it is written, Eye hath not seen, nor ear heard, neither have entered into the heart of man, the things which God hath prepared for them that love Him.*

From Grieving to Grateful

Even though I was not ready to leave Heaven, and I had to return to wake up out of the coma; there were a lot of people interceding on my behalf and praying for my breakthrough. I found out much later that when I first went into my coma, my husband had called all of our ministerial friends and asked them to pray for us. Out of all of our friends, there were a couple of people who took that extra step to reach out and do more than pray. Bishop

Leonard Scott and First Lady Christine Scott, with whom I worked for at a gospel recording company called Tyscot Records, were the first to come out to the hospital where I was and laid hands on me. I found this ironic because for years Sis. Scott was my prayer partner at Tyscot. We would intercede for our families, the company, and artists that we produced. My prayer language grew every time I prayed with her. I believe she was one who helped take my ministry of intercession to another level of growth and now she was interceding for me. That was just another sign that God was with me. The Scotts were and continue to be righteous people, and I believe that one of the many reasons I am still here is because the prayers of the righteous availed much. I know God blessed me with righteous people to pray for me when I couldn't pray for myself. I like to call them generals and veterans in the faith, and they bombarded Heaven on my behalf. For that, I am continually grateful.

Earlier, I introduced my spiritual parents, Pastor Bob and Martha Ruth Kirkley, another couple who were there for us in our time of despair. While I was in intensive care, they had come in my room to pray for me. While Pastor Bob started warring in prayer against the spirit of bitterness, the very thing I told you I believed to be the beginning cause of my sickness, all the machines in my room started going off. The nurses came in and made Pastors Bob and Martha Ruth Kirkley leave because they thought they were upsetting me, but it was the enemy who was upset. He was upset because our pastors were calling out what he was trying to use to defeat me, which was bitterness, and it is like rottenness to the bones. The damage had already been done; his plan had already been ruined. I had a whole army of righteous women and men of God who refused to see me taken down. The pastors and members of Immanuel House of Prayer, the church we belonged to at the time, were always praying for us and interceding on our behalf. I know that it is because of those prayers and the healing power of God that I am healed this very day.

Thinking of all those who helped me during this time, I can't help but recall when my husband and I both really needed prayer. While I was still in a coma, the doctors had decided to put me on a ventilator, and on that day my husband had to make a very tough decision. Pastors Bob and Martha Ruth Kirkley and Elder Ronald and Sis. Cathy Tucker were there to be our support system. My husband will tell you, even with their support, it was the hardest thing he had to do, but their presence definitely made the process easier. My husband always says that Elder Tucker gave him the best advice to help him through, to read Psalm 25 every day and to be encouraged that Jesus would make a way. That is exactly the advice that my husband took, and he was able to stand even stronger.

From Failure to Favor

It was during the time I was incubated that my husband and I were extremely blessed. Due to my hospitalizations all the time and my husband being the loving man he is, trying to be with me every step of the way; my husband took a leave of absence from his job which only gave him a partial salary. Our house went into foreclosure due to this financial strain and our closest friends knew this. So, on Father's Day, the men of Immanuel House of Prayer came to be with my husband at the hospital and be a comfort to him. While there, they presented us with a love offering of over one thousand dollars. This was so overwhelming to us since we didn't have enough money to cover our miscellaneous bills, much less our mortgage. The love shown to us during this time was priceless, and my husband appreciated it with all of his heart. We will be forever grateful to all those who helped us. We were blessed, and the three years that I was in and out of the hospital, we did not pay a mortgage payment. Our house did not get foreclosed until after my third hospital stay and after I began walking in my healing. I will share more on that miraculous story in a later chapter. We actually lived out the scripture Psalm 37:25, *I have been young and now am old; yet have I not seen the righteous forsaken, nor his seed begging bread.*

From Hurt to Hope

Blessings were not only given to us during this time, but also our children. They were suffering as well from being at the hospital for long periods of time because they were kids and full of energy. The hospital was not a place for them to release their energy or to have any amount of recreation, but as my youngest daughter Jasmine will tell you, they made the best of it. They would bring sleeping bags to the hospital and play like they were camping, and I remember them walking all around the hospital finding what they called "secret spots" that they probably weren't suppose to be in. Somehow, they found a route that took them from the heart hospital to the main hospital I was staying at. I was moved around quite a bit from the heart hospital, to critical care, to intensive care, to a regular room. Even though everyone who worked there knew their names and who they were, I still don't know how they were able to do all that running around without anyone saying anything to them. Workers in the cafeteria would even give them free food sometimes. My children were the "hospital kids", and though they made the best of it, I could not stand to see them suffer. I prayed that the Lord would give them some type of recreation so they wouldn't have to be there 24/7.

My oldest daughter Jennifer did not like to come in my hospital room because it scared her to see me so sick. However, when she did come in she would bring me things, most of the time another Bible because I had a tendency to read and write in them so much that they would fall a part. I was surprised to find in one of the Bibles a letter to God she had placed in it that read, "God please heal my mom so she can come home with us," and that really touched my heart. I was so hurt that my children were experiencing all this, but all I could do was pray the same prayer Jennifer had and believe that God would move. I hoped in my heart that God would bless my children.

One day my husband Derrick came to the hospital to sit with me, but the kids were not with him. So I asked him, "Honey, where are the kids?"

He told me he had let them stay home with the neighbors because they had got a pool in their backyard, and they said the kids could come over and swim whenever they wanted to. I was amazed. I had been praying for our children to be blessed with some type of recreation, and God did just that for them. I believed he had placed it in our neighbor's heart to get a pool in their backyard just to bless our children. I was so happy and thankful God blessed my children right when they needed it most, and I know they were happy too. They went swimming every day, would come visit me in the evenings, and spend the night at the hospital in the lobby, while my husband was with me in my room. My children Jennifer, Derrick Jr., and Jasmine were one of the main reasons why I fought so hard to live. I love them with all my heart and they are a blessing to my husband and I beyond words. They have made us so proud, and God made them little soldiers through this whole ordeal. I call them my Three Musketeers, God's Infantry Soldiers. I thank God for the family he has blessed me with, especially my mother-in-law that encouraged my husband and I daily. I recall every Tuesday after her choir rehearsal at church; she would call to let me know that her and the choir prayed for me and wished me well. A true saying I held onto from a little girl says, "A family that prays together, stays together," and God has truly kept us together through prayer.

From Suffering to Survival

Though we were happy with all the love and prayers we were receiving, the enemy certainly was not. He tried a method he had used before, but this time more intensely which made the hospital a place of suffering for me. When I came out of my coma, I was constantly deprived of the attention needed for someone who was in such critical condition. I give God glory for the doctors and nurses that took good care of me, but I can not be remiss about the share of neglect while I was in the hospital for those forty days. With constant bowel movements that I had no control of, I was quite embarrassed, and I cried a lot because I was not use to having someone take care of me in this manner. I can recall many days when one particular nurse was on duty and would rarely check on me. When she did, she would not clean me up, so I would lay there in my mess. It seemed like she would wait until my husband was gone to neglect taking proper care of me in a timely manner. To complicate matters more, due to being bed ridden and in a coma, I laid on my back side for a long period of time and it resulted in me having really bad bed sores, which were so painful that I cried daily. The nurse was suppose to turn me over often and medicate the sores, but she didn't do that either. Fortunately for me my sister-in-law Minister Shaya Rowe, whom I've known since she was four years old, would show up at the hospital every time I had been laying there suffering in that mess and pain. It seemed like God would speak to her and have her come and check on me. She took care of me, cleaning me up immediately, and I was so thankful that God sent her each time. I love her dearly, and I am forever grateful for her.

From Fear to Faith

By having an encounter with God, reading my bible, and praying all the time, I knew the reason this nurse was acting like this and being neglectful in her job was due to the fact that she was being used by the enemy to make me suffer even more. Satan knew I would be a righteous ambassador for Christ when I survived this ordeal. True, I didn't want to leave God's presence in Heaven, but when Jesus told me I had to come back and that I would be fine here on earth that ended all the fear I had in me. After that, I knew I was not going to die, but live and declare the works of the Lord. The scripture I held onto after I came back from Heaven is Psalm 118:17 - I *shall not die, but live, and declare the works of the Lord.* God had said that I would do great things for Him here on earth, and I believed Him because whatever God speaks shall come to pass. God always confirms His will for our lives. God spoke to me often in dreams and visions, but I will never forget how he spoke to me through my first pastor, Pastor Clifton Russell, who was then pastor of Gabriel Missionary Baptist Church. He came to visit me on day 38 of my 40 day stay in the hospital.

When Pastor Russell came in he said, "Sis. Carpenter, God said Rise Up and Walk!" We use to sing a song at Gabriel years ago called "Rise Up and Walk" by Reverend Milton Brunson.

When he spoke that, something in my spirit awakened and I felt empowered like never before. The very next day, the doctors came to check my vital signs, and they were shocked to see that everything was returning to normal. In two days my blood pressure was stable, I had no fever, my bowels were normal again, the swelling in my brain had completely gone down, and my kidneys were stabilizing.

I received that Word from God in my spirit, so my body had to line up according to the Word of God. It was time; He wanted me to "Rise Up and Walk", and just like Lazarus in the Bible I did just that. That stay in the hospital changed my life. My faith walk became more stable, my spiritual discernment increased, my ability to see into the spiritual realm intensified, and my physical healing began to take its complete course. To this day, I know that God was with me through it all! I understand now why God said some people will not be saved, healed, and delivered unless I go back to the earth and speak what he tells me. I witnessed the power behind speaking what God tells you to speak. Many people prayed for me while I was in the hospital the third time, and that sustained my life. But, I did not rise up until Pastor Russell, who was my first Spiritual Father, came and spoke what God told him. It was only when He spoke those words from God that I felt empowered to rise above my bed of affliction. That day, I learned the importance and value of having spiritual parents. They have the key to unlock your destiny. I will talk about this more in the chapters to come, but remember, it is extremely essential for you to know who your spiritual parents really are.

Chapter Three

HEALING AT HOME

From Heartache to Healing

In 2001, after my forty day stay at the hospital, I was finally released to go home. Before I knew it, time had passed quickly and it was Thanksgiving. I felt so dejected because I was still bed ridden and unable to cook our family Thanksgiving meal, which I did every year. Fortunately, I had taught our oldest daughter Jennifer how to cook at an early age, and I called her upstairs and asked her did she think she could cook, since I was still unable to move. Having been bed ridden for so long, I needed to strengthen my limbs and learn to use them all over again. She was up for the challenge! They went to the store and shopped for everything a person would need for an awesome Thanksgiving Dinner, and when the food was done, I was so proud of her because she successfully cooked an entire Thanksgiving meal. It tasted just as good, if not better, than my own cooking.

Along with the good days came some bad days as well. Although I was home and beginning to walk in my healing, some things still reminded me that the enemy had not given up. One day while sitting on my shower seat, since I still couldn't stand by myself, the chair seat slipped out from under me. It somehow ended up on top of me and had pinned me in the shower. I was stuck and could not get up. The water from the shower drenched me, while screaming my oldest daughter's name for help. The more I cried out for help the more the water was pouring into my mouth. I felt like I was drowning and could not lift myself up out of the water; I was too weak. It seemed like someone was holding me down and pouring tons of water down my throat and nose like water boarding; which is what they use to torture prisoners. I knew that I was wrestling with a demon sent by the enemy to kill me. There was no reason at all for that chair seat to just slip out from underneath me, but it did. Jennifer had just put me in the shower, so she was right downstairs, but for some reason she could not hear me for at least five minutes. When she finally came to my rescue, she possessed enough strength to pick me up from under the seat and save my life. God corrected me after this incident because I use to get on Jennifer about her weight all the time. She had started to gain weight, and I didn't want her to be unhealthy, so I would tell her she needed to watch her weight. After what happened in the shower, God told me to never talk about her weight again. If she hadn't been that size, she would not have had the strength or weight to lift me up from underneath that shower chair.

Then, another incident occurred around the Christmas holiday when I had started to get my strength back in my limbs and began to walk again. My husband and I had went to the supermarket to get some items for Christmas and do a little walking, though I was still quite tired and weak. While there, I started feeling sick in my body, but I felt I would make it because I had seen and felt worse days. Around this time, I was having what doctors called hallucinations, and I found myself getting paranoid, thinking I was going to die. As soon as the thought entered my mind, a woman with a demonic spirit came right up to my face like she was going to hit me and spoke out loud what I was thinking in my head. In a demonic voice she said, "I am so tired, I'm just about to die."

I fought off being scared and paranoid, because I knew what I was dealing with. The enemy wanted me to believe I was crazy, but I knew that I was really spiritually in tune with God, especially after my encounter with Him during my coma. The woman turned and walked away, and I immediately started praying. I found my husband, who was in another aisle, and I told him that we needed to leave because I was beginning to feel bad. We left, and I felt better after I got in the bed and had my husband lay hands on me in prayer. I thank God for my husband; he was a real trooper through all of this. I am forever grateful to God for Pastor Derrick S. Carpenter Sr., a mighty man of Valor. Only God knows what he went through during this whole ordeal.

From Mess to Miracle

In the midst of my encounters, God began to move. All the despair I was feeling, while going through my complete healing, began to leave because I could finally feel myself slowly getting better. The decree of the Lord that Pastor Russell had given me when I was released from the hospital to "Rise Up and Walk" was coming into full fruition.

Soon after being home from the hospital, a leader of the congregation at Immanuel House of Prayer, Minister Gerald Jones, gave my husband Derrick a bottle of Tahitian Noni Juice. He encouraged him to give it to me because it was known for healing many conditions. I started drinking the Noni Juice and began to feel better and stronger in my body each day. This reminded me of the scripture Ecclesiastes 2:5 - *I made myself gardens and orchards, and I planted all kinds of fruit trees in them.* Over the course of three months, my symptoms and issues had completely disappeared. This included my kidneys, which were close to failure, and doctors thought only dialysis could help. Jeremiah 30:17 - *For I will restore health unto thee, and I will heal thee of thy wounds saith the Lord.* I had regained my strength and got my life back again! I completely attribute this to God's healing power through His Word, fasting, prayer, and a healing fruit created by God just for me called Noni, which means "Miracle Gift". My doctors were stunned and absolutely amazed by my progression. They told me whatever I was doing that I needed to keep doing it, and that is exactly what I did. My doctors did not know that I also had started the process of weaning myself off of the twenty-two medications they had put me on. I don't suggest anyone do this because it can be quite dangerous, but I did because I believe I was being instructed by God on how to walk in my healing for a complete recovery. Since then, I have not taken any of those medications, chemotherapy, or dialysis, with the exception of a low dose of blood pressure pills. I believe God to be off of those this year.

Back to Gabriel M.B Church: From Offenses to Obedience

While back at home in 2002, we decided to leave Immanuel House of Prayer and return to Gabriel, the church where it all began. The reason we did this was because The First Lady, Sis. Mollie Russell had passed and God told us to go back to our home church, and serve our spiritual father, where I had been since I was 10 years old. During the time we came back to our home church, we had a meeting with Pastor Russell where we told him we felt like God was calling us to pastor and launch a new work to start a church. But, before we did this, we first had to come back and serve. Pastor Russell agreed and said that if we came back and helped him, he would bless us out when God said it was time.

While at Gabriel for the second time, we learned what true obedience was. Pastor Russell use to tell me all the time, obedience is better than sacrifice. This held a lot of truth for me because we really didn't want to go back to what we felt was traditional, but God had already been working behind the scenes. He had been preparing Pastor Russell's heart to receive me as a woman in ministry. God had given me the testimony that Pastor Russell had just told me years earlier I needed to have. Now, while back under the covering of Gabriel Missionary Baptist Church, I was licensed by my pastor to preach the Gospel. I have always been twenty years ahead of time, but twenty years ago, when I first knew I was called to preach, this would not have been possible, but God was making me a tradition breaker. My husband and I were both allowed to preach and minister while serving our pastor faithfully until he passed away in 2005. I am so happy we obeyed God even when it was uncomfortable, because that's what opened the door for our blessings to begin flowing. It was a blessing and a true honor to have served Pastor Russell the last three years we were there. We have great and wonderful memories that we will cherish for a lifetime, and we are looking forward to spending eternity with him and First Lady Mollie Russell in heaven.

After Pastor Russell passed, I had a dream that my husband and I were sitting side by side in two big high back burgundy chairs. Pastor Russell came and laid hands on both of us and blessed us, and then he released us to start a new work for the Lord. He gave us this big smile that only he could give; Pastor Russell had the nicest smile in the world. I woke up with tears of joy, knowing that we had his blessing. I told my husband, and we both knew it was time for God's will to be done in our life. The Faith Church is now the distant dream that had come true. I will share in chapters to come the testimony of how The Faith Church was birthed after we were blessed by Pastor Russell in my dream.

Chapter Four

ALL ABOUT THE FAMILY

From Moods to Memories

Although my body was healed, I still had withdrawals from all of the medications that were in my body, which resulted in lots of mood swings. The doctors had never instructed me to stop taking the twenty-two medications they gave me, but as I revealed, I had begun to wean myself off of them because they were making me mentally and emotionally sick. In order to stop myself from this type of behavior, I chose to focus on positive memories. This kept me in a positive and upbeat mood as I reflected on how much God had blessed me. My whole life is a testimony, and even before the sickness, I knew God was with me when I was just a little girl.

When I was born on December 16, 1962, as an only child to Elizabeth A. Beeler and James O. Smith, it was right after my grandmother died. My birth brought new life to my family after the loss they had experienced, and it also filled the void that was in their hearts. Because of this, I found favor with them, especially my grandfather Vernon Beeler. We were really close, and my mom and I lived with him up until I was 8 years old. When we finally moved from his house, I became very sad because we did everything together. He taught me how to drive his red pickup truck, how to farm, how to drive a tractor, and also how to cook. He would play the guitar and banjo for me, and this began my love for music. He bought me anything I could have ever imagined I would want, and he was the best grandfather anyone could have asked for. He also hosted the family fish fries, holiday dinners, and parties. He meant the world to me. When he died I was about ten years old, and a part of me died with him. For years I felt a big void in my life, but all that changed when I met Jesus and made Him my personal Savior.

After my grandfather passed away, my Aunt Lucille and I, who was my mother's oldest sister, became even closer. She was a role model for me all my life and she taught me about God at the early age of 5 or 6. She was the "church lady" of the family, and she kept most of the children on the weekends so that she could take us to church, Sunday School, and Vacation Bible School. This is where I first learned to love God and His word and began to express a desire to sing in the choir. My Aunt Lucille sang and had a beautiful voice, so I wanted to do the same thing. I looked forward to the Sundays that she would sing one of my favorite solos, "He touched me and He made me whole", not realizing this song would one day be my testimony and that He would touch my body and heal me; which made me whole. Although Aunt Lucille is now gone home to be with the Lord, I wrote her this poem in her honor:

AUNT LUCILLE

A HIGHLY RESPECTED LADY

To My Aunt Lucille; May I say you're a Highly Respected Lady

You're always there, showing you care to your family, friends, and grand-babies

You're always running here and there, lending a helping hand

And trying to teach others about God's Word and His commands

You are that special person the family listens to

And whenever there's a problem, the family calls on you

I often wonder how you stay strong, and accept the responsibility

Of all the ones who count on you, to help them in time of need

But I guess you are that special one, which God has made of gold

For you have all the goodness in your heart, and many treasures
you hold

And I will never ever forget, the words you told me one day

Never lay your head to rest, before you look to God and pray

So when I have my family, I'll pass it down to them

That Aunt Lucille always said, put God before all men

And when you lay your head to rest, always say your prayers

Even if it's simple like, Thank You Jesus, I love you, Amen...

So my Dear Auntie, again I'd like to say,

You're a Highly Respected Lady, in each and every way

I thank you for your guidance; I thank you for your love

Most of all I thank you for bringing me close to our Father above.

****

Another dear memory of mine was of my mother and the time we spent together while she was alive. Every Thursday, when my mom got paid, I would meet her downtown after she got off work and she would take me to Ted's Steak House. They had the best steak and salad in the world to me. I loved how she took time out of the week, outside of being at home, to spend time with me. I will always treasure those Thursday outings with just us two. I didn't know it then, but she was instilling me with memories I would need to lean on for comfort when she passed away. I still cherish every moment my mother and I shared together, and I tell mothers all the time to spend time with your children because when they are young they are on your lap, but when they are old they are on your heart. Mothers should impart as much as they can to their children while they are young. My pastor use to say, "The hand that rocks the cradle, rules the world."

I have fond memories of my mom during the Christmas Holiday. My love for Christmas Carols is largely because every year my mom would break out her Christmas albums, particularly Mormon Tabernacle Choir "Oh Holy Night". This was one of my favorite songs because my mom loved it and sang it all the time. My mom was so wonderful in my eyes because she taught me so much. I remember my mother buying a Bible story series from a door to door salesman. They had pictures and Bible stories in them, and I would read a Bible story just about everyday. I learned about Adam and Eve, David and Goliath, Jonah and the Whale, Jesus & His Disciples, and many more.

My mother was everything to me and I truly adored her because she sacrificed so much for me so I could have a wonderful childhood and life. My mom was and still is my Hero or "Shero", and since I was an only child that made us even closer. I expressed her importance to me through this poem:

THANKS MOMMA

You gave me so many things

The hopes and dreams of what life would bring

You taught me how to handle myself

Who to trust and who to put upon a shelf

You gave me love so strong and warm

It kept me safe away from harm

Then for me you did something else

You let me stand all by myself

You gave me enough strength to know

That I could stand once you let go

You gave me courage enough to try

To learn to walk and hope to fly

You let me make decisions for myself

Even when you knew my decisions were not the best

You sacrifice so much for me

You gave me a chance to stand and be free

Thanks Momma for all you've done, Because of you, I'm whole I'm

One...

With love, Your One and Only Daughter

Lauren Denise Smith Carpenter

****

Another memory I have is one that I will never forget, and

that memory is of my dad. My earliest memory of my father was around four or five years of age. Because my mom and dad were never married, I did not really build a close relationship with him until I was a pre-teenager, and at the age of 18, which was my senior year in high school, he died of cancer. Though he had accepted Christ at an early age, just as my mother had, they both didn't come back to Christ until their later years in life. I remember visiting my father one day at the hospital, and he told me to get back in someone's church. At the time I was not attending church on a regular, and I knew I needed to get back into it. My dad was so sincere when he spoke those words, it seemed like his eyes were speaking without a sound. After he passed, I wrote a poem about something left unspoken in his eyes, but now I understand what it was. It was the love of God pleading with me to come back to him and serve him like I did when I was a little girl. When he passed, I went back to church as he instructed, and have been in church ever since. I was eighteen when this happened, and now at fifty years old I am still serving the Lord thirty-two years later because my father gave me the best advice any father could have ever given a child, and that advice was to come back home to God. I plead with fathers to make sure they give their children sound advice and leave them with a solid foundation, which is Jesus Christ. One word from a father can change a child's destiny, and a father's blessing is important to a child. Fathers please bless your children with a committed life in Christ. I am so thankful to my father for speaking those words into my life. I wrote this poem for my father:

DADDY

SO MUCH LEFT UNSPOKEN IN YOUR EYES

Daddy that day you laid on your dying bed, I wish I knew what your eyes had said

For they were gleaming out at me, with love so warm like a bright shining beam

Oh Daddy I wish I knew then, what your eyes spoke before you entered in

Oh Daddy I wish I could turn back time, to let you know I got back

in line

Your dying words pierced my heart, it changed my life, and I made

a new start

Oh Daddy you'd be so proud of me, I'm saved, healed, and I'm set

free

I know you're waiting up there for me

And when that time comes your eyes I will see

This time Daddy I do understand, what your eyes spoke was God's

love for man.

****

My paternal grandmother was an angel from above, I loved
her so much. She had such an inner strength that laid a strong
foundation for our family. This kept us close in heart even when we
were apart from each other. She was an amazing woman of God
whom I adored. I wrote this poem for her when my grandfather

(Paw Paw) died because he kept the family laughing and brought us joy. I would like to share her poem with you:

GRANDMOTHER

GOD BLESS YOU DEAR MAW MAW

God Bless you dear Maw Maw, for your love and tender care

When days become dark and hopeless, you were always willing and there

God bless you dear Maw Maw for your faithful loyal love

I know you are an angel, God has sent from Heaven above

Your never ending vigil, through sorrow and through tears

You stood by in trying times, your mate of many years

Although we loved Paw Paw dearly, and wanted him here evermore

It was God's will for him to go, for our Father loved him more

God Bless you dear Maw Maw, and though you two had to part

Paw Paw will live forever, in good memories and in your heart

So may your days be brighter, in everything you do

I love you dear Maw Maw, and may GOD BLESS YOU.

****

When I recall all the wonderful memories of my childhood and all the wisdom that was spoken to me back then, it helped me make it when I thought I didn't have the strength to. Thinking about all the strong women in my life made me realize that I could be strong as well, especially with God on my side. Now, my family and I are walking in complete victory!

From Grief to Growth

Though my family went through many struggles and changes during the time I was sick at the hospital, and even while at home recovering, we made it through with God. Joel 2:25-26 – *And I will restore to you the years that the locust hath eaten the canker worm and the caterpillar, and the palmerworm, my great army which I sent among you. And ye shall eat in plenty and be satisfied and praise the name of the Lord your God that hath dealt wondrously with you; and my people shall never be ashamed.* These scriptures have proven true for us. While still recovering and beginning to walk in my complete healing, my oldest daughter Jennifer got pregnant out of wedlock. Needless to say, our relationship was a little strained because of this situation, but God restored it. Jennifer ended up marrying the father of her first child, who submitted his life to Christ and is now a minister at our church. They also have four beautiful children together. Even in this blessing, God still caused us to work our faith. Serenity, their second oldest child, passed away at seven months old from SIDS (Sudden Infant Death Syndrome). Though grief stricken, her parents and the rest of the family kept the faith and praised the Lord through it all. We stood on God's Word in Romans 8:28 - *All things work together for the good to them that love the Lord and are called according to His purpose.*

Reflecting back on our home of many years that we lost to foreclosure, we had lived there while I was in the hospital, unable to pay a mortgage for those three years, and that can only be contributed to the favor of God. When we finally had to move out of the house, it was our decision to start over because we were so far in the rear to refinance, so we let it go. The miracle in the house story is: A man around the corner from our home that we lost purchased the house for little of nothing out of foreclosure. He was going to resale it and make a profit. Our neighbors next door knew the man that bought the house and they called and told us. We called the man and told him our testimony and how God told us to ask him to rent our house back to us for one year, and then we would get a loan and buy it back from him. He did not hesitate to do exactly what we asked of him.

He said, "With a powerful testimony like that and the pictures to back your story is all I need to know. God is with you, this is your house, and you can have it back."

Not only did we get our house back, we got a check back for $17,000 because the house had equity in it. We still live in the house today.

Then, there was the lost of my husband's job, but together with our oldest daughter, we started a daycare business called Little Angels Christian Daycare. The youth ministry we had founded while working with inner-city children recorded a CD and became a national recording choir called The Jesus Gang. Our children recorded several CD projects entitled *Gospel Kids*, all this under Tyscot Record Label, the oldest and largest black owned gospel record company in the country. Today, we have a youth choir called New Generation of Praise and a praise team called P.R.A.I.S.E., who is now in the process of releasing Gospel CD's. Everything has come full circle! We give God the glory for what He has done, and for blessing us to be able to still work with all His beautiful children. This is a poem I wrote for all the children God has blessed me to work with now and over the years:

NO MORE BURIED TREASURES

Too many talents have been hidden and buried

Too many gifts have simply gone astray

Too many treasures have been lost and stolen

These treasures are the children of today

It's time to take a stand and say

No more treasures Satan get away

It's time to take a stand and say

No more buried treasures today

He's buried our children spiritually

They're just bodies walking around dead

He's buried our children physically

Too many lying in their grave bed

It's time to take a stand and say

No more treasures Satan get away

It's time to take a stand and say

No more buried treasures today

My family and I have been through more than many could ever imagine, and some things God would not allow me to share in this book, but I thank the Lord for every experience high and low. I never pass up the chance to praise the Lord for all the things He has done for me, my family, and our ministry.

Chapter Five

LOOKING FORWARD TO SEEING YOU AGAIN

From Pain To Praise

Earlier I shared about my second oldest grand-daughter passing in her sleep. Serenity was seven months old when she left this earth to be with our King Jesus. She was so young, and it seemed her life ended before it could even begin. She was beautiful; she had a peace about her and her eyes spoke wisdom like she had been on earth before. We believe she was a little angel sent by God, but even in this ordeal rested a word from God. We never know how much time we have, and I believe my grand-daughter was a blessing. She came to bring joy, happiness, and to teach us to be grateful for each second we are alive. She fulfilled her purpose because now, everyone in the family does just that. After Serenity passed, nine months later Jennifer birthed our third grand-daughter named Miracle, and what a miracle it was. God was still in the blessing business, and He restored what we thought was lost. Miracle is another sign from God that He was with us against all odds.

I've always found something ironic about Serenity passing in her sleep because she was not the first one. As I said before, my mother also passed in her sleep along with my brother-in-law Dax. Death is seen as sad, depressive, and extremely hard to cope with for the family involved. I am often asked how I was able to cope with the death of my family members passing in their sleep, and I always respond that I learned to turn my pain into praise. With each of my family members passing in their sleep, it was not easy, but accepting death had a peace about it now, and my ability to cope would become increasingly stronger. When my mom died, I almost died from bitterness and grief. However, when my brother-in-law Dax passed at fourteen years old, and later my seven month old grand-daughter Serenity, I turned my pain into praise. I immediately turned on praise and worship music all over the house and just gave God as much glory as I could. Why not? Serenity, Dax, and my mom all made it to a place that we all long to go and hear our Lord and Savior say, "Well done". A place I saw with my own eyes while on my death bed; a place and person that I fought so hard to be able to preach about. A place filled with love, peace and, happiness, not filled with darkness, hate, and violence that we constantly deal with on a daily basis here on this earth. They are finally free in Heaven with our Father the Lord Jesus Christ. I have hope in my heart because I know I will see them again. It's not goodbye, it's see you later for those who have accepted The Lord Jesus Christ as their personal Savior. 1st Thessalonians 4:13 - *But I would not have you to be ignorant, brethren, concerning them which are asleep, that ye sorrow not, even as others which have no hope.* Our family learned a valuable lesson about passing in your sleep. Never go to bed mad, and always tell your loved ones you love them because someone may not wake up the next day. We live by this rule to this day, and it has brought us much closer as a family. Ephesians 4:26 - *Be angry and sin not, don't let the sun go down on your wrath.*"

Chapter Six

CALLED AND CHOSEN

From Crisis to Courage

Things were definitely starting to look up for me on the ministry side. My ordeal forced me to increase my faith in God on a deeper level. I knew for a long time that God wanted to use me in the area of preaching, but knowing that some people wouldn't come to Christ unless I did what He asked me to do gave me more reasons to press. As the Word says, many are called but few are chosen, and God had chosen me. My confidence was boosted, my head was held high, and I was ready to be completely sold out for what the Lord wanted me to do. Matthew 20:16 - *So the last shall be first, and the first last; for many are called, but few chosen.* Wow! God had put me in the front of the line. After twenty years of hearing God call me to preach the gospel, it was now time for the gift to come forth in me.

On September 7, 2003, the day I was given my license from Pastor Russell at Gabriel Missionary Baptist Church, I became a tradition breaker; I felt that Pastor Russell and I had been obedient to what God wanted to happen. Like I stated before, this had never been done in Gabriel. I was the first woman to get a license, and I felt honored. God wanted that tradition to be broken and he chose me to break it. For His word says, *My sons and my daughters shall prophecy*, Joel 2:28.

For this sermon, I preached a message titled, "Against All Odds" influenced by my life and 2nd Timothy 2:1-3 – *You then, my son, be strong in the grace that is in Christ Jesus. And the things you have heard me say in the presence of many witnesses entrust to reliable people who will also be qualified to teach others. Join with me in suffering, like a good soldier of Christ Jesus*. In this scripture, grace means strength. When I was going through my sickness, and the odds against me said I would die, I had to be strong. But, the strength inside me wouldn't have been enough because according to all doctor records, I was extremely weak.

However, I was strong in the strength that is in Christ Jesus. I drew as much as I could from Jesus through prayer, fasting, reading the Word, applying it through dedication, and also through believing in the call He placed on my life. Without the Lord's strength, there is no way I would have survived because the odds were not in my favor.

Another part of this message that spoke volumes, as it relates to my life, was the word qualified. For a long time, since I was both a woman and didn't have a big enough testimony, I was viewed as unqualified for such a task as preaching and being a woman pastor was out of the question. But God knew that He could entrust me with His word and His people. He knew I would be reliable and faithful in giving His love and His message to His people; He qualified me. I believe I became qualified through my suffering. A lot of people view suffering as a negative thing, but I have learned that it is only through suffering for Christ sake that you can receive your crown. To this day, I still get frowned on by tradition for being a woman pastor, but I am reminded of the scripture in Galatians 6:17, *From henceforth let no man trouble me; for I bear in my body the marks of the Lord Jesus.*

A General Gone Home: From Tears to Thanksgiving

In 2005, before Pastor Russell went home to be with the Lord, God's Word was brought to pass. He said, "Pastor Russell's heart would be changed in believing and accepting women preachers," and that is exactly what happened. When asked what I believe was the spiritual reason behind my sickness, I respond, "To be a tradition breaker and to birth the pastor in me".

Before, I was more afraid of man than God. I didn't want to leave Gabriel when I did because I had been there since I was ten years old, and I loved my church dearly. I came to Gabriel through a childhood friend at school, Gail Elaine Russell Freeman. Back then, the church was called Guiding Light, and Gail's father was the pastor. After he passed, her uncle Pastor Clifton Russell took the church, and years later we became Gabriel. I remember Gail coming to school singing, "It's Gonna Rain," and because I loved to sing and by my Aunt Lucille planting Godly seed in me at an early age, I wanted to sing with her about the Lord. Gail's mother, Sis. Geraldine Russell Ford began picking me up for choir rehearsal, Bible Class, and Sunday Morning Service just like my Aunt Lucille had done when I was younger. She and the entire Russell family adopted me as one of their own. I had been with them for many years, so I did not want to leave because we were family. Then when I left, I didn't want to go back when God told me to because I thought I would be shut down and not able to minister in the Word of God like I was at previous churches. It was an unwilling transition, but I knew since God said it I had to do it. Transition is dangerous all by itself and along with the benefits comes new challenges and tests. However, transition without God's guidance or self-will is even worse; it was a battle I was not willing to fight. True, when I did what God said and left Gabriel, I got hit pretty badly, but obedience and following God's every word spared my life. If I hadn't done that, the enemy would've been able to defeat me. The same is true if we had not gone back to Gabriel in obedience to the voice of God; we would have been defeated.

Ultimately, we obeyed God's voice, so now we walk in victory, and

our once doubts about ministry have become dreams that have

come true. We give God all the glory.

Chapter Seven

THE FAITH CHURCH

From Doubts to Dreams

After Pastor Russell passed, we went into prayer and fasting. We talked with several pastoral friends of ours, and they confirmed what we knew God was speaking to us about launching a new work. During our time of prayer and fasting, God instructed us to contact Pastor's Bob and Martha Ruth Kirkley and ask for a meeting to discuss our next step. God showed up at the meeting and confirmed to us that the Kirkleys, who are now our spiritual parents, were to be our covering. We were to be ordained under their Apostle Jeff Johns and join the fellowship at White Horse Christian Center. Pastor Carpenter was already an ordained minister, but they felt God wanted us both to be ordained together under the same covering since, we would be pastoring together as a team. Well we did what God said, and words cannot express how we have been blessed by connecting to our covering that God had chosen for us. The Kirkleys were God sent, to say the least, and I can write an entire book on how God has used them to be a blessing to us and so many others that they touch with God's love on a day to day basis. It is so important to be connected to whom God has chosen for you. They hold the key to your destiny, and only that key will unlock the door to your true destiny that God has for you. The Kirkleys unlocked the door to our next level in God, and we are so grateful for them, Apostle Jeff & Sis. Jane Johns, and The White Horse Christian Center Family for their love, guidance, and support. To God be the glory for the things He has done.

In 2005, my husband Pastor Derrick and I launched a new work in ministry. We are now the proud pastors of The Faith Church in Indianapolis, Indiana, where *We Walk by Faith and not by Sight*, 2 Corinthians 5:7. God has blessed us with a wonderful church family full of young people whose hearts are on fire for the Lord; reminding us of ourselves years back when we started serving the Lord. We teach them to love the Lord with all their heart, soul, mind, to walk in obedience, and always pray. We teach them to never pass up the opportunity to praise Him for being God all by Himself. We always share with them our testimony of making it through our test, trials, temptations, and tribulations by showing faith in God. We are so grateful to God for choosing us to declare His works, and all we can say is to God be the glory for the things He has done.

Originally, the name of our ministry was Faith Full Gospel Church, and it began on March 13, 2005, at a hotel called the Econo Lodge. When the ministry started there were 29 partakers, we now have over 200 partakers on our roster. We held Sunday Morning Services at Econo Lodge, and choir rehearsal, Bible Study, and Friday Night Prayer Services were held at our business location Little Angels Christian Daycare, which was a blessing from God being that I use to work at the same building for Tyscot Records. Now, the same facility I use to work at was housing our business and would soon house our new church. We began to grow rapidly, and as God blessed us, we were able to expand and knock down walls at the daycare location. With God's continued blessings, our first Sunday Service at the daycare location was on May 1, 2005. God had blessed us with a building large enough to house the business and the church. To God be the glory.

Now, The Faith Church is still growing strong, and in 2010 the Lord blessed the Faith Church to expand and knock more walls down to edify our sanctuary. On March 14, 2010, we dedicated our new sanctuary along with celebrating our 5th year Church Anniversary. We are excited about our ministry's future, and we are looking forward to the great things God has called us to do for Him. We want to make a difference as our mission statement says by, *"Exalting the Savior, Evangelizing the Sinner, Equipping the Saints, and Empowering Society."*

We are now in prayer for a youth center for the children in our inner city called "The Ark of Safety". We are diligently praying it to come into fruition so our inner city children can have a safe environment to learn about God, with recreation and fun. This center, connected to the church, will redirect youthful lives away from the threats of idleness, delinquent, and elicit behavior, and redirect them towards high self-esteem, and positive productive behavior. Our unique approach towards reaching this generation is in operation now at the facility we are in. We desire to expand into one-facility equipped to meet every physical, spiritual, social, and educational need that our young people have. We will extend the hours of our current daycare to a twenty-four hour daycare facility for young parents to have a place where their children can be nurtured and trained in a Godly and trusted atmosphere. We are firm believers that our youth don't need a definition of religion and tradition, but they need a demonstration of God's love.

I remember when Jesus told me I had to go back for my children, other children and people He would send my way to minister to. I now understand the assignment now and the need to have a safe environment for our children and young people. God said it and I believe it shall come to pass. I have seen God do so much in my lifetime that there is nothing I won't believe Him for. If God said it, that settles it. I am so grateful and honored when I think about how God chose me for such an awesome task for end time ministry, tears swell up in my eyes. I give God the glory for sparing my life for His work.

At The Faith Church, we have a lot of different opportunities and vehicles of worship you can use to draw closer to God. Our worship will help you focus on God, our fellowship will help you face life's problems, and our discipleship will help fortify your faith. Our ministry also helps you find and develop your gifts; while our evangelism will help you fulfill your mission. We will continue to walk by faith and not by sight; trusting that God will fulfill our destiny in Him.

From Problems to Promotion

One of the things we aim to instill in our church is that God is able to save us from our addiction to sin. One of my favorite movies is <u>Lady Sings the Blues</u>, featuring Diana Ross and Billy Dee Williams. The movie portrays the story of Billie Holiday who was a drug addict; she was addicted to heroine. The addiction she had reminds me of how we have become addicted to the things of the world such as, TV, social networks, drugs, alcohol, sex, and much more. My favorite part of the movie is when Billy Dee held out his hand to her and she did not respond. He asked her, "Are you just gonna stand there and let my hand fall off?" Then, he waited on her to make a choice.

This reminds me of how God is always reaching out to us. His arms are stretched wide open for us to make a choice and come to Him just as we are, but we stand there waiting to make a decision. The longer we wait, the more indecisive we become. Jesus is coming back, and you have to know this day where you will be going when he comes, so don't procrastinate. The time is now to accept Him as your personal Savior.

I would like to take this time and extend an opportunity for you to accept Jesus as your personal Savior if you do not know the man I have been talking about in the previous chapters. If you are willing to pray the sinner's prayer with me, you can be saved right now while reading this book. Please pray this prayer out loud:

Salvation Prayer

Heavenly Father, I pray this prayer as an act of belief to Romans 10:9 which says, *If you confess with your mouth the Lord Jesus, and believe in your heart that God has raised Him from the dead, you will be saved.*

In Jesus' Name, I repent of my sins and open my heart to let you come inside of me. I believe that You are the Lord Jesus Christ. Jesus, You are my Lord and Savior. I believe you died for my sins and you were raised from the dead. Cleanse me with your blood and fill me with Your Holy Spirit.

Thank you Father for saving me, in Jesus' Name, Amen.

From Overload to Overcoming

The Faith Church is the church of more than enough. That is not just something we declare, but it is a reality for us. Our church and the people in it always have what they need and more. God's favor rests with us in every season of our lives, and for that we are thankful. Everything anyone could possibly need is IN THE HOUSE! Here's a list of some of our ministries:

- Little Angels Christian Daycare

- Sunday School

- Sunday Morning Worship

- Wednesday Night Bible Study/Christian Education

- Friday Night Intercessory Prayer

- P.U.S.H. Pray Until Something Happens

- Choir/Music Ministry

- P.R.A.I.S.E.

- Youth & Dance Ministry

- H.Y.P.E. Holy Youth Pursing Excellence

- Young Ladies of Virtue

- Daughters of Destiny

- Men's Fellowship (Man Up Ministry)

- Missionary/We Care Outreach Ministries

- Evangelism/Love Outreach

- God's Soup Kitchen

- God's Storehouse

- Marriage Counseling /Extra Ordinary Marriage

- Prison Ministry/Substance Abuse Program (Journey to Freedom)

The Faith Church is a soul winning church as you see. We want to do the will of God in these last days and bring souls to Christ, while advancing the Kingdom of God. So whatever way God blesses us to do this, we will use. Our mission as I stated before at The Faith Church is:

Exalting the Savior,

Evangelizing the Sinner,

Equipping the Saints,

And Empowering Society

THE FAITH CHURCH DECLARATION PRAYER

The Faith Church is the church of more than enough spiritually, physically, financially, and laughingly.

We are living a life of overflow blessings.

We are blessed in the city, we are blessed in the field, we are blessed when we come and when we go.

In Jesus' Name

We Are Blessed

TO GOD BE THE GLORY

Chapter 8

AGAINST ALL ODDS TESTIMONY PICTURES

DIAGNOSIS AND SYMPTOMS

Organs Shutting Down

Epileptic Seizures

Blood Pressure 218/190

Loss use of all limbs

Paralyzed with pain

Cancerous Cells

Lupus

Rheumatoid Arthritis

Abrasions all over body

Aids (Impossible)

Kidney Failure

Coma

Dialysis

Ventilator

Irregular Heartbeats

After a 40 day hospital stay, I was sent home with 22 Medications,

scheduled for chemotherapy and dialysis.

Romans 8:38

I am persuaded that neither death

nor life shall be able to separate us from

the love of God.

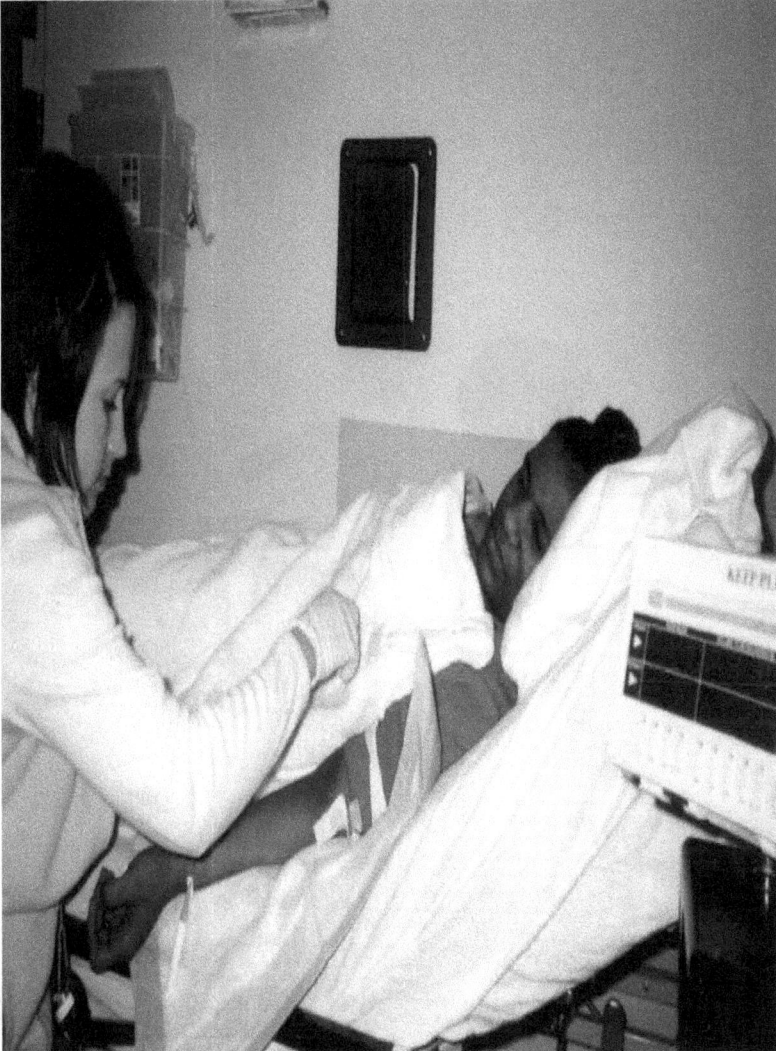

Psalm 27:13

I had fainted unless I had believed to see the goodness of the

Lord in the land of the living.

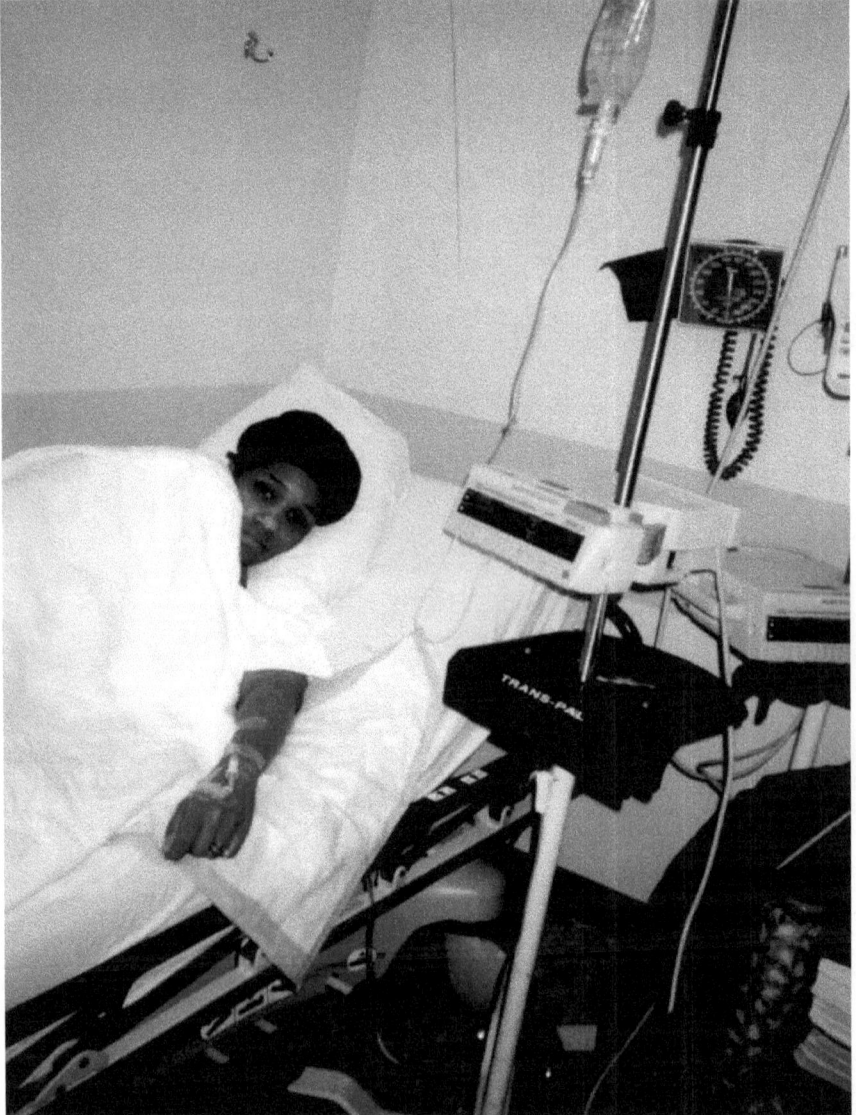

Romans 8:37

Nay in all these things we are more than conquerors

through him that loved us.

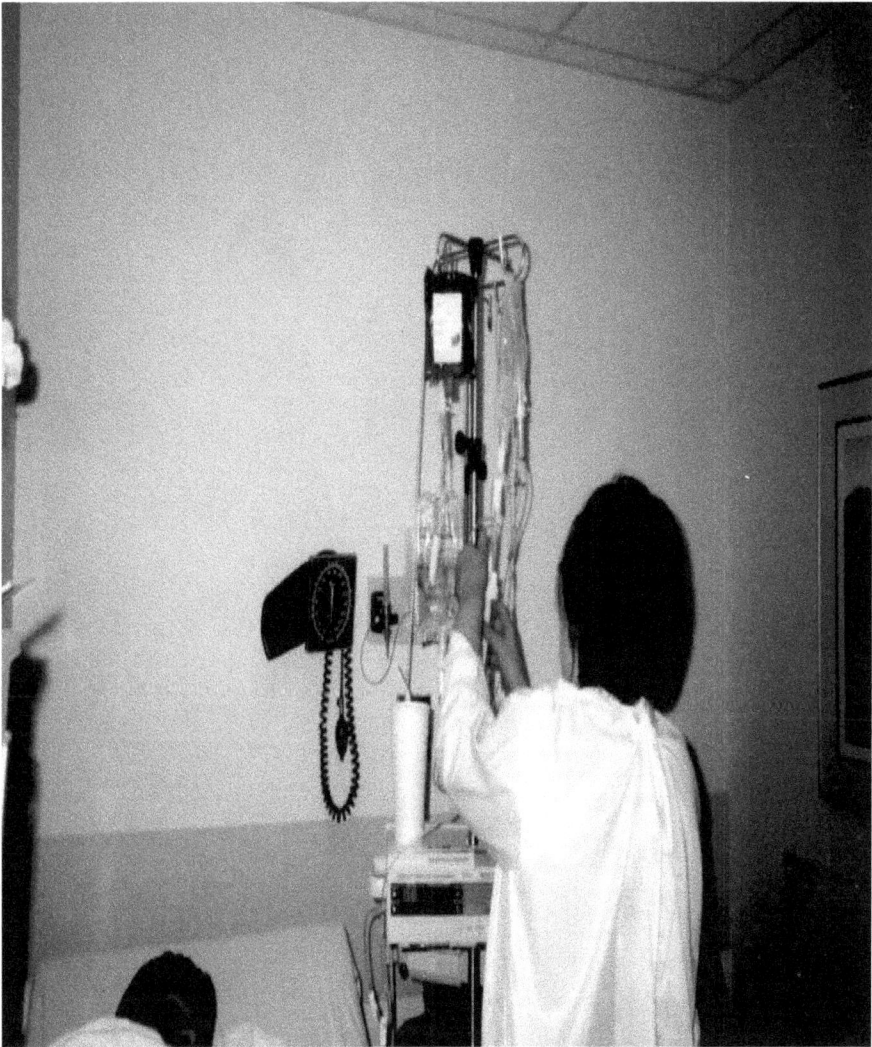

Psalm 12:1

Help Lord!

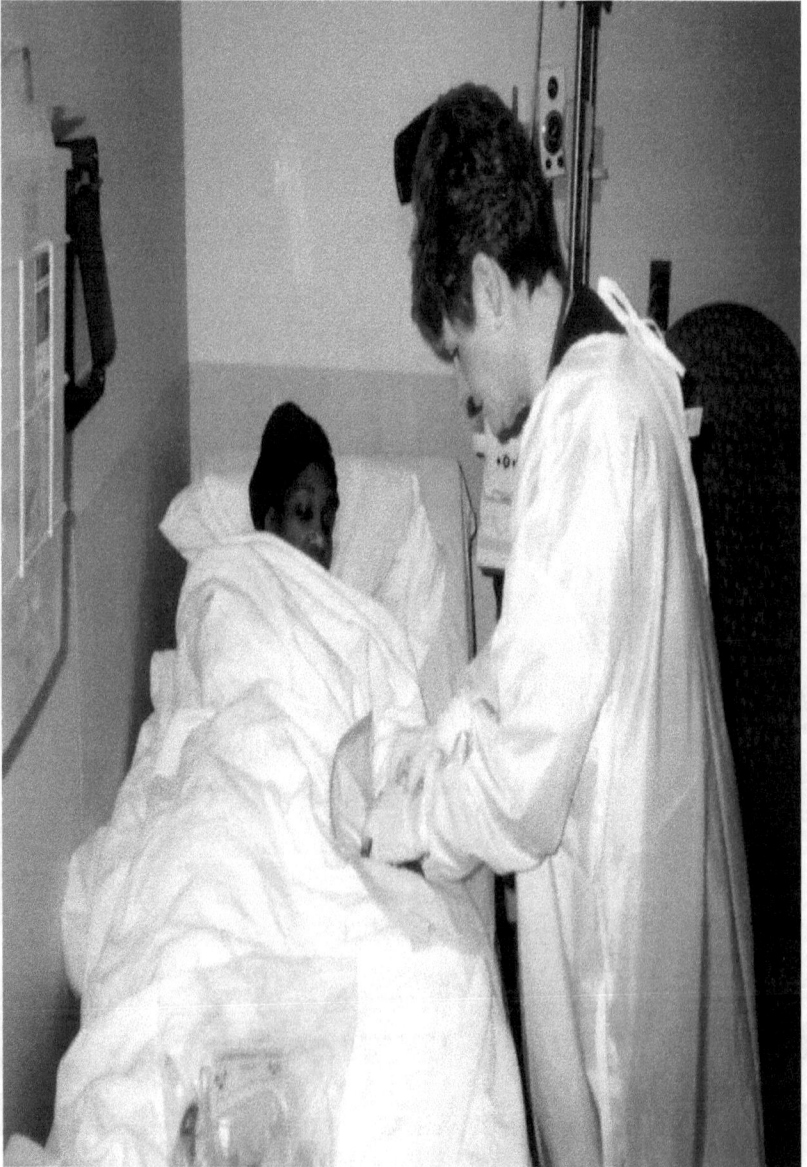

Psalm 18:4

The sorrows of death compassed me.

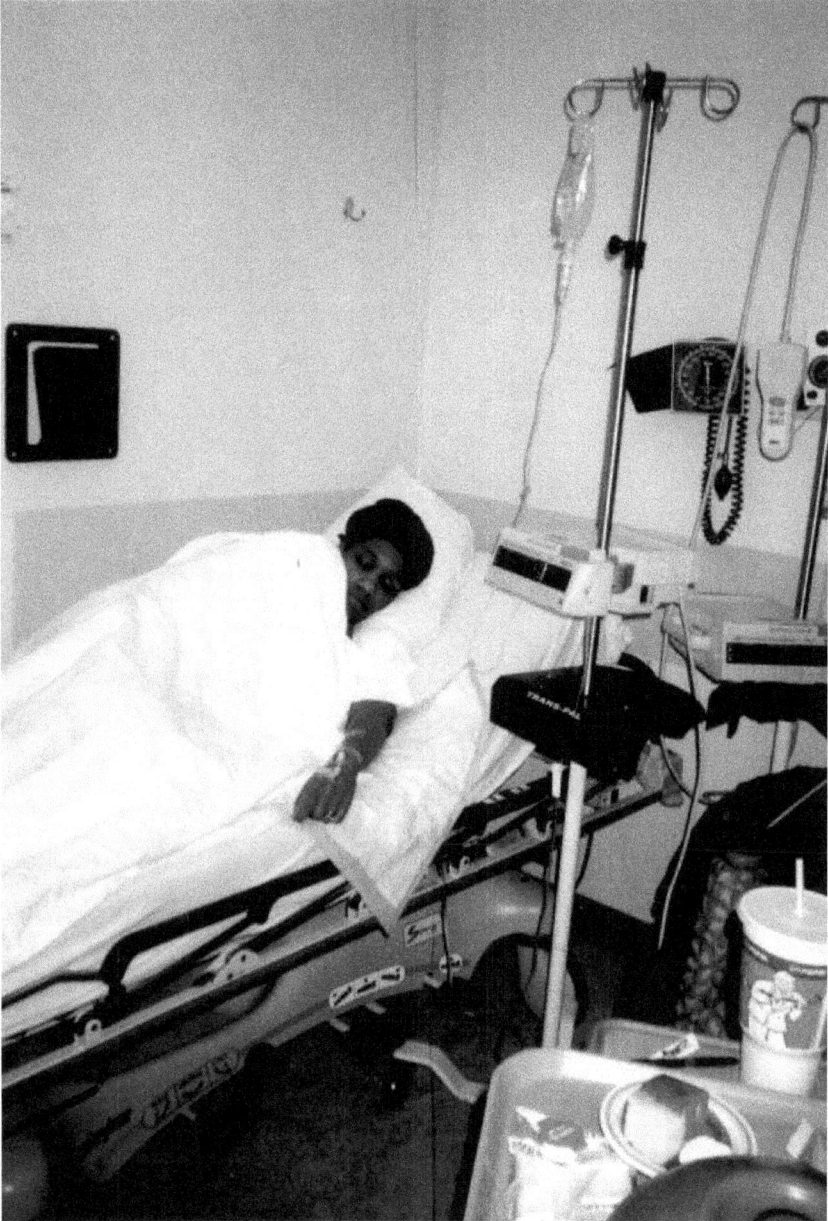

James 5:16

The effectual fervent prayer of a righteous man availeth much.

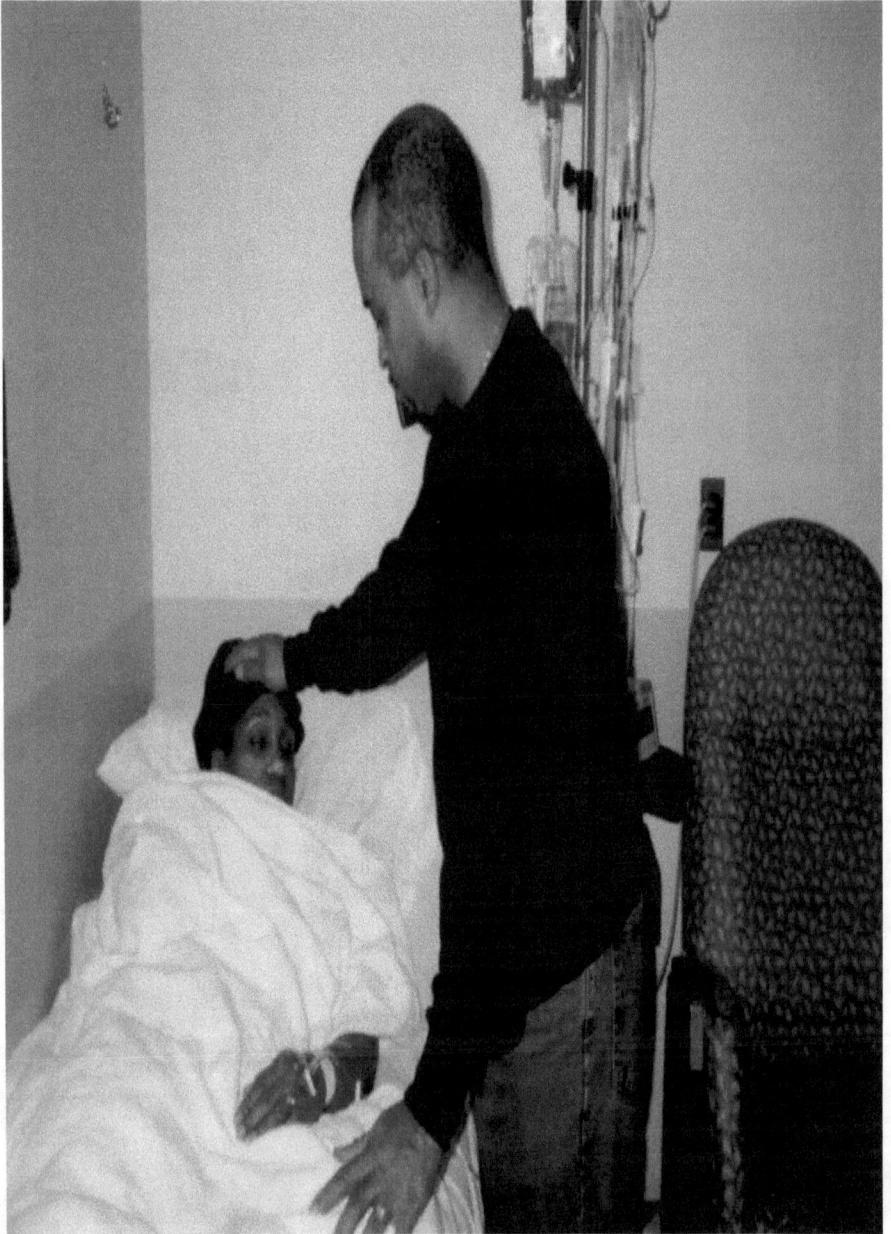

1 Peter 2:24

By Jesus stripes I am healed.

"I beat the odds"

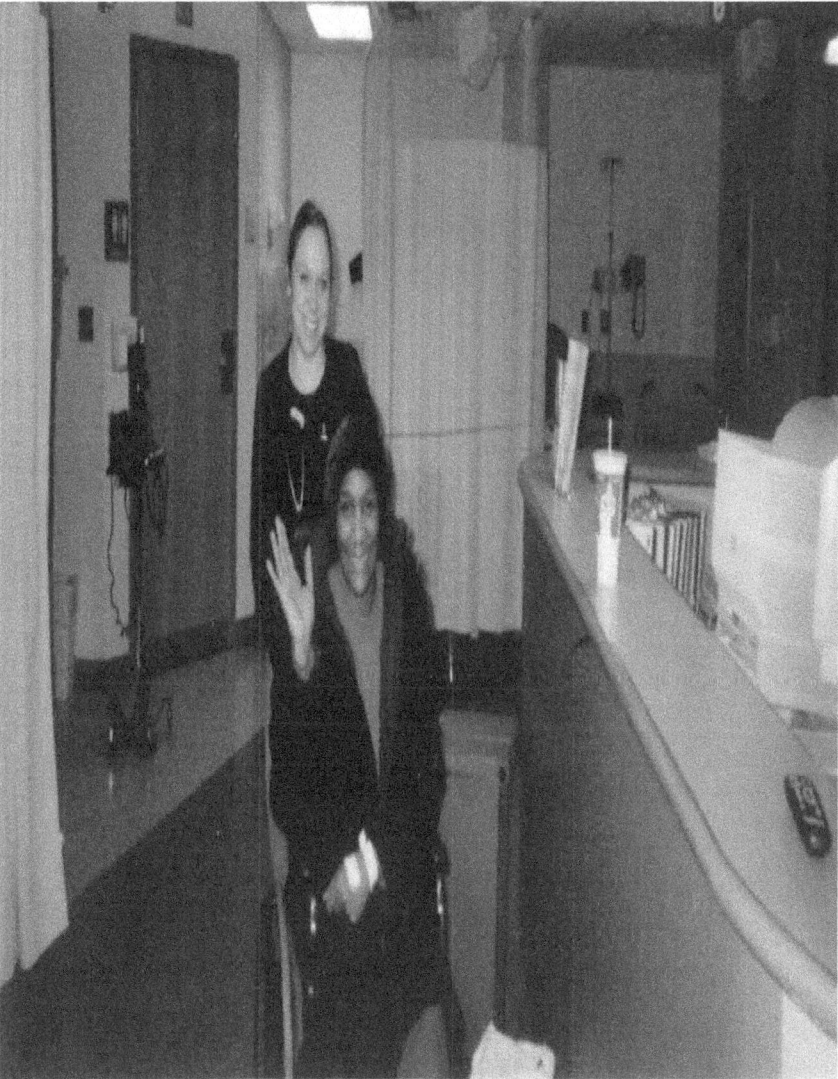

Romans 8:18

For I reckon that the suffering of this present time are not

worthy to be compared with the glory that will be revealed in

us.

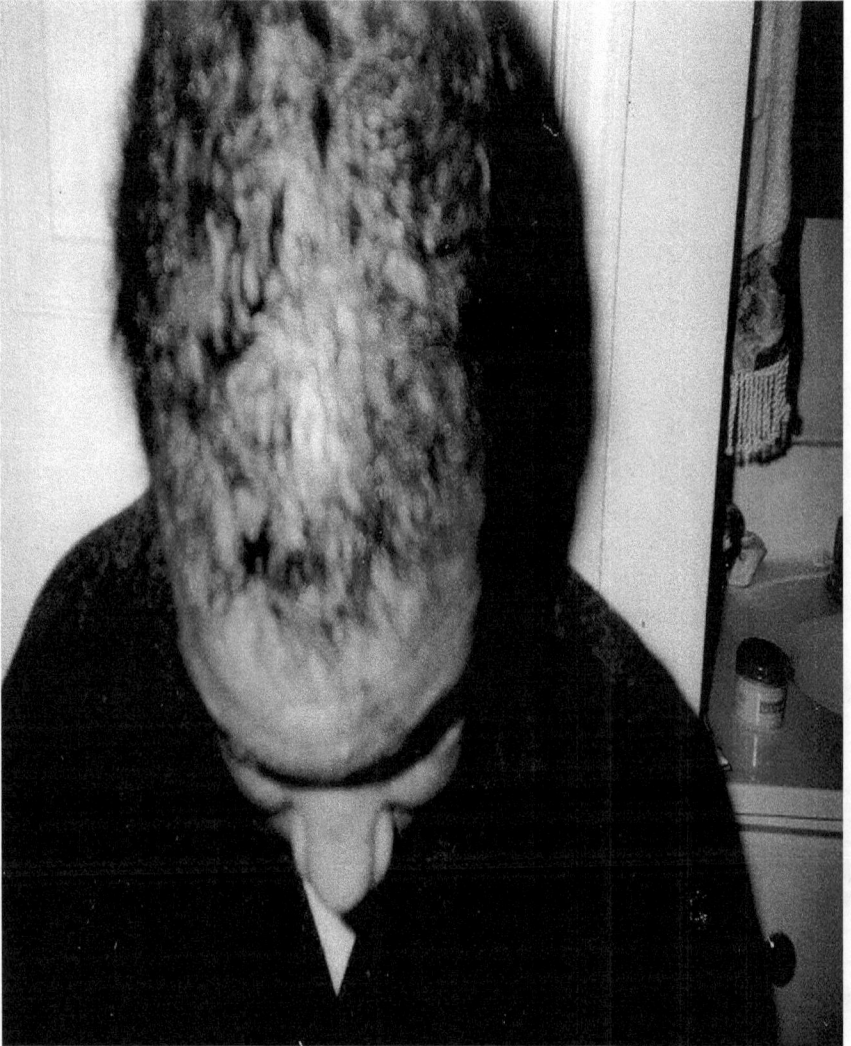

Psalm 121:1

I will lift up mine eyes unto the hills from whence cometh my help. My help cometh from the Lord who made heaven and earth.

Proverbs 17:22

A merry heart doeth good like a medicine: but a broken spirit drieth the bones.

Psalm 119:71

It is good for me that I have been afflicted that I might learn

thy statues.

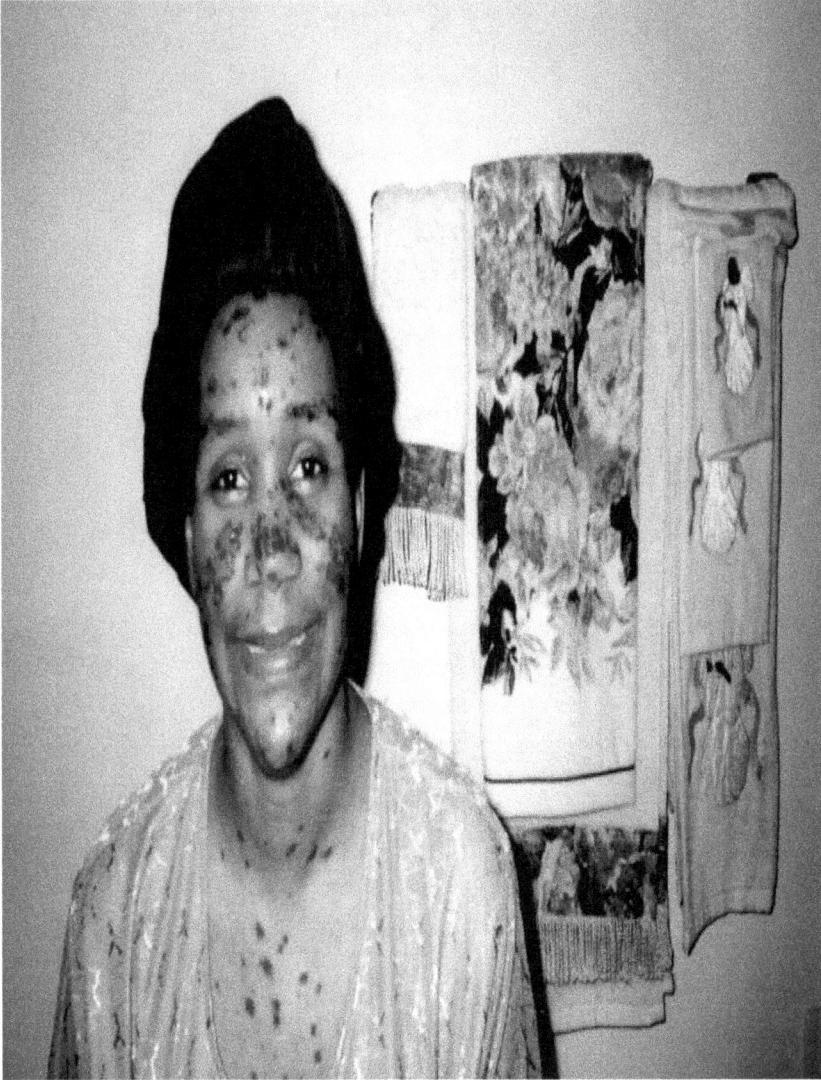

Nehemiah 8:10

The joy of the Lord is my strength.

After 3 months of drinking Tahitian Noni Juice!

I began walking in my healing.

Ecclesiastes 2:5

I made me gardens and orchards, and I planted trees in them

of all kinds of fruits.

To Purchase Noni Juice go to:
http://www.mymorinda.com/2575652/en-us/store/tahitiannoni/index.html

A family that prays together stays together.

THE PASTORS PRAYER

Dear Lord,
We thank you for the honor of being
A Shepherd for Your people
We thank You for the life experiences
That have prepared us for this call
For every trial, for every tribulation,
And everything we've suffered so that
 We would learn to obey you....
We thank You

We thank you for giving us a
Heart for your people
For empowering us to empower them
For bringing us out so that we
Can guide them through
For breaking us so that
We can speak healing over them

Lord because it is not we that live
But You that live in us we declare that
When they are lost
We will go and find them
When they are burdened
We will share their yoke
When they feel unloved
We will love them
When they fall we will pick them up
We will always give the truth
That You have given us
And that truth will make them free

Chapter 9

AGAINST ALL ODDS FAVORITE SCRIPTURES

Romans 8:38-For I am persuaded that neither death nor life, nor angels nor principalities nor powers, nor things present nor things to come.

Psalm 27:13-I would have lost heart, unless I had believed that I would see the goodness of the Lord in the land of the living.

Psalm12:1-Help, Lord, for the godly man ceases! For the faithful disappear from among the sons of men.

James 5:16-Confess your trespasses to one another, and pray for one another, that you may be healed. The effective, fervent prayer of a righteous man avails much.

1 Peter 2:24 -Who Himself bore our sins in His own body on the tree, that we, having died to sins, might live for righteousness by whose stripes you were healed.

Proverbs 17:22-A merry heart does good, like medicine, But a broken spirit dries the bones.

Psalm 121:1-I will lift up my eyes to the hills from whence comes my help?

Romans 8:18-For I consider that the sufferings of this present time are not worthy to be compared with the glory which shall be revealed in us.

Psalm 119:71-It is good for me that I have been afflicted, that I may learn Your statutes.

Nehemiah 8:10-Then he said to them, "Go your way, eat the fat, drink the sweet, and send portions to those for whom nothing is prepared; for this day is holy to our Lord. Do not sorrow, for the joy of the Lord is your strength."

1 Corinthians 15:54 -So when this corruptible has put on incorruption, and this mortal has put on immortality, then shall be brought to pass the saying that is written: "Death is swallowed up in victory."

1 Corinthians 15:57 -But thanks be to God, who gives us the victory through our Lord Jesus Christ.

Psalm 118 -Oh, give thanks to the Lord, for He is good! For His mercy endures forever. 2 Let Israel now say, "His mercy endures forever." 3 Let the house of Aaron now say, "His mercy endures forever." 4 Let those who fear the Lord now say, "His mercy endures forever." 5 I called on the Lord in distress; The Lord answered me and set me in a broad place. 6 The Lord is on my side; I will not fear. What can man do to me? 7 The Lord is for me among those who help me; Therefore I shall see my desire on those who hate me. 8 It is better to trust in the Lord than to put confidence in man. 9 It is better to trust in the Lord than to put confidence in princes. 10 All nations surrounded me, But in the name of the Lord I will destroy them. 11 They surrounded me, Yes, they surrounded me; But in the name of the Lord I will destroy them. 12 They surrounded me like bees; They were quenched like a fire of thorns; For in the name of the Lord I will destroy them. 13 You pushed me violently, that I might fall, But the Lord helped me.

14 The Lord is my strength and song, And He has become my salvation. 15 The voice of rejoicing and salvation is in the tents of the righteous; The right hand of the Lord does valiantly. 16 The right hand of the Lord is exalted; The right hand of the Lord does valiantly. 17 I shall not die, but live, And declare the works of the Lord. 18 The Lord has chastened me severely; But He has not given me over to death. 19 Open to me the gates of righteousness; I will go through them, And I will praise the Lord. 20 This is the gate of the Lord, Through which the righteous shall enter. 21 I will praise You, For You have answered me, And have become my salvation. 22 The stone which the builders rejected has become the chief cornerstone. 23 This was the Lord's doing; It is marvelous in our eyes. 24 This is the day the Lord has made; We will rejoice and be glad in it. 25 Save now, I pray, O Lord; O Lord, I pray, send now prosperity. 26 Blessed is he who comes in the name of the Lord! We have blessed you from the house of the Lord. 27 God is the Lord, And He has given us light; Bind the sacrifice with cords to the horns of the altar. 28 You are my God, and I will praise You;

You are my God, I will exalt You. 29 Oh, give thanks to the Lord, for He is good! For His mercy endures forever.

Psalm 18 -I will love You, O Lord, my strength. 2 The Lord is my rock and my fortress and my deliverer; My God, my strength, in whom I will trust; My shield and the horn of my salvation, my stronghold. 3 I will call upon the Lord, who is worthy to be praised; So shall I be saved from my enemies. 4 The pangs of death surrounded me, And the floods of ungodliness made me afraid. 5 The sorrows of Sheol surrounded me; The snares of death confronted me. 6 In my distress I called upon the Lord, And cried out to my God; He heard my voice from His temple, And my cry came before Him, even to His ears. 7 Then the earth shook and trembled; The foundations of the hills also quaked and were shaken, Because He was angry. 8 Smoke went up from His nostrils, And devouring fire from His mouth; Coals were kindled by it. 9 He bowed the heavens also, and came down with darkness under His feet. 10 And He rode upon a cherub, and flew; He flew upon the wings of the wind. 11 He made darkness His secret place; His canopy around Him was dark waters and thick clouds of the skies.

12 From the brightness before Him, His thick clouds passed with hailstones and coals of fire. 13 The Lord thundered from heaven, and the Most High uttered His voice, Hailstones and coals of fire. 14 He sent out His arrows and scattered the foe, Lightnings in abundance, and He vanquished them. 15 Then the channels of the sea were seen, The foundations of the world were uncovered At Your rebuke, O Lord, at the blast of the breath of Your nostrils. 16 He sent from above, He took me; He drew me out of many waters. 17 He delivered me from my strong enemy, From those who hated me, For they were too strong for me. 18 They confronted me in the day of my calamity; But the Lord was my support. 19 He also brought me out into a broad place; He delivered me because He delighted in me. 20 The Lord rewarded me according to my righteousness; According to the cleanness of my hands He has recompensed me. 21 For I have kept the ways of the Lord, And have not wickedly departed from my God. 22 For all His judgments were before me, And I did not put away His statutes

from me. 23 I was also blameless before Him, And I kept myself from my iniquity. 24 Therefore the Lord has recompensed me according to my righteousness, According to the cleanness of my hands in His sight. 25 With the merciful You will show Yourself merciful; With a blameless man You will show Yourself blameless; 26 With the pure You will show Yourself pure; And with the devious You will show Yourself shrewd. 27 For You will save the humble people, But will bring down haughty looks. 28 For You will light my lamp; The Lord my God will enlighten my darkness. 29 For by You I can run against a troop, By my God I can leap over a wall. 30 As for God, His way is perfect; The word of the Lord is proven; He is a shield to all who trust in Him. 31 For who is God, except the Lord? And who is a rock, except our God? 32 It is God who arms me with strength, And makes my way perfect. 33 He makes my feet like the feet of deer, And sets me on my high places. 34 He teaches my hands to make war, So that my arms can bend a bow of bronze. 35 You have also given me the shield of Your salvation; Your right hand has held me up, Your gentleness has made me great. 36 You enlarged my path under me, So my feet did not slip. 37 I have pursued my enemies and overtaken them; Neither did I turn back again till they were destroyed. 38 I have wounded them, So that they could not rise; They have fallen under my feet. 39 For You have armed me with strength for the battle; You have subdued under me those who rose up against me. 40 You have also given me the necks of my enemies, So that I destroyed those who hated me. 41 They cried out, but there was none to save; Even to the Lord, but He did not answer them. 42 Then I beat them as fine as the dust before the wind; I cast them out like dirt in the streets. 43 You have delivered me from the strivings of the people; You have made me the head of the nations; A people I have not known shall serve me. 44 As soon as they hear of me they obey me; The foreigners submit to me. 45 The foreigners fade away, And come frightened from their hideouts. 46 The Lord lives! Blessed be my Rock! Let the God of my salvation be exalted. 47 It is God who avenges me, And subdues the peoples under me; 48 He delivers me from my enemies. You also lift me up above those who rise against me; You have delivered me from the violent man. 49 Therefore I will give thanks to You, O Lord, among the Gentiles, And sing praises to Your name. 50 Great deliverance He gives to His king, And shows mercy to His anointed, To David and his descendants forevermore.

Psalm 77 -In Judah God is known; His name is great in Israel. 2 In Salem also is His tabernacle, And His dwelling place in Zion. 3 There He broke the arrows of the bow, The shield and sword of battle. Selah 4 You are more glorious and excellent than the mountains of prey. 5 The stouthearted were plundered; They have sunk into their sleep; And none of the mighty men have found the use of their hands. 6 At Your rebuke, O God of Jacob, Both the chariot and horse were cast into a dead sleep. 7 You, Yourself, are to be feared; And who may stand in Your presence when once You are angry? 8 You caused judgment to be heard from heaven; The earth feared and was still, 9 When God arose to judgment, To deliver all the oppressed of the earth. Selah 10 Surely the wrath of man shall praise You; With the remainder of wrath You shall gird

Yourself. 11 Make vows to the Lord your God, and pay them; Let all who are around Him bring presents to Him who ought to be feared. 12 He shall cut off the spirit of princes; He is awesome to the kings of the earth.

Psalm 67 -God be merciful to us and bless us, And cause His face to shine upon us, Selah 2 That Your way may be known on earth, Your salvation among all nations. 3 Let the peoples praise You, O God; Let all the peoples praise You. 4 Oh, let the nations be glad and sing for joy! For You shall judge the people righteously, And govern the nations on earth. Selah 5 Let the peoples praise You, O God; Let all the peoples praise You. 6 Then the earth shall yield her increase; God, our own God, shall bless us. 7 God shall bless us, And all the ends of the earth shall fear Him.

Psalm 23-The Lord is my shepherd; I shall not want. 2 He makes me to lie down in green pastures; He leads me beside the still waters. 3 He restores my soul; He leads me in the paths of righteousness For His name's sake. 4 Yea, though I walk through the valley of the shadow of death, I will fear no evil; For You are with me; Your rod and Your staff, they comfort me. 5 You prepare a table before me in the presence of my enemies; You anoint my head with oil; My cup runs over. 6 Surely goodness and mercy shall follow me All the days of my life; And I will dwell in the house of the Lord Forever.

Psalm 25 -To You, O Lord, I lift up my soul. 2 O my God, I trust in You; Let me not be ashamed; Let not my enemies triumph over me. 3 Indeed, let no one who waits on You be ashamed; Let those be ashamed who deal treacherously without cause. 4 Show me Your ways, O Lord; Teach me Your paths. 5 Lead me in Your truth and teach me, For You are the God of my salvation; On You I wait all the day. 6 Remember, O Lord, Your tender mercies and Your loving kindnesses, For they are from of old. 7 Do not remember the sins of my youth, nor my transgressions; According to Your mercy remember me, For Your goodness' sake, O Lord. 8 Good and upright is the Lord; Therefore He teaches sinners in the way. 9 The humble He guides in justice, And the humble He teaches His way.

10 All the paths of the Lord are mercy and truth, To such as keep His covenant and His testimonies. 11 For Your name's sake, O Lord, Pardon my iniquity, for it is great. 12 Who is the man that fears the Lord? Him shall He teach in the way He chooses. 13 He himself shall dwell in prosperity, And his descendants shall inherit the earth. 14 The secret of the Lord is with those who fear Him; And He will show them His covenant. 15 My eyes are ever toward the Lord; For He shall pluck my feet out of the net. 16 Turn Yourself to me, and have mercy on me, For I am desolate and afflicted. 17 The troubles of my heart have enlarged; Bring me out of my distresses! 18 Look on my affliction and my pain, And forgive all my sins. 19 Consider my enemies, for they are many; And they hate me with cruel hatred. 20 Keep my soul, and deliver me; Let me not be ashamed, for I put my trust in You. 21 Let integrity and uprightness preserve me, For I wait for You. 22 Redeem Israel, O God, Out of all their troubles!

Healing Scriptures

Exodus 15:25-26 –So he cried out to the Lord, and the Lord showed him a tree. When he cast it into the waters, the waters were made sweet. There he made a statute and an ordinance for them, and there He tested them, 26 and said, "If you diligently heed the voice of the Lord your God and do what is right in His sight, give ear to His commandments and keep all His statutes, I will put none of the diseases on you which I have brought on the Egyptians. For I am the Lord who heals you."

Exodus 23:25-So you shall serve the Lord your God, and He will bless your bread and your water. And I will take sickness away from the midst of you.

Deuteronomy 7:15 -And the Lord will take away from you all sickness, and will afflict you with none of the terrible diseases of Egypt which you have known, but will lay them on all those who hate you.

Deuteronomy 28:1-14,61-"Now it shall come to pass, if you diligently obey the voice of the Lord your God, to observe carefully all His commandments which I command you today, that the Lord your God will set you high above all nations of the earth. 2 And all these blessings shall come upon you and overtake you, because you obey the voice of the Lord your God: 3 "Blessed shall you be in the city, and blessed shall you be in the country. 4 "Blessed shall be the fruit of your body, the produce of your ground and the increase of your herds, the increase of your cattle and the offspring of your flocks. 5 "Blessed shall be your basket and your kneading bowl. 6 "Blessed shall you be when you come in, and blessed shall you be when you go out. 7 "The Lord will cause your enemies who rise against you to be defeated before your face; they shall come out against you one way and flee before you seven ways. 8 "The Lord will command the blessing on you in your storehouses and in all to which you set your hand, and He will bless you in the land which the Lord your God is giving you. 9 "The Lord will establish you as a holy people to Himself, just as He has sworn to you, if you keep the commandments of the Lord your God and walk in His ways. 10 Then all peoples of the earth shall see that you are called by the name of the Lord, and they shall be afraid of you. 11 And the Lord will grant you plenty of goods, in the fruit of your body, in the increase of your livestock, and in the produce of your ground, in the land of which the Lord swore to your fathers to give you. 12 The Lord will open to you His good treasure, the heavens, to give the rain to your land in its season, and to bless all the work of your hand. You shall lend to many nations, but you shall not borrow. 13 And the Lord will make you the head and not the tail; you shall be above only, and not be beneath, if you heed the commandments of the Lord your God, which I command you today, and are careful to observe them. 14 So you shall not turn aside from any of the words which I command you this day, to the right or the left, to go after other gods to serve them. 61 Also every sickness and every plague, which is not written in this Book of the Law, will the lord bring upon you until you are destroyed.

Deuteronomy 30:10-20 -If you obey the voice of the Lord your God, to keep His commandments and His statutes which are written in this Book of the Law, and if you turn to the Lord your God with all your heart and with all your soul. 11 "For this commandment which I command you today is not too mysterious for you, nor is it far off. 12 It is not in heaven, that you should say, 'Who will ascend into heaven for us and bring it to us that we may hear it and do it?' 13 Nor is it beyond the sea, that you should say, 'Who will go over the sea for us and bring it to us that we may hear it and do it?' 14 But the word is very near you, in your mouth and in your heart, that you may do it. 15 "See, I have set before you today life and good, death and evil, 16 in that I command you today to love the Lord your God, to walk in His ways, and to keep His commandments, His statutes, and His judgments, that you may live and multiply; and the Lord your God will bless you in the land which you go to possess. 17 But if your heart turns away so that you do not hear, and are drawn away, and worship other gods and serve them, 18 I announce to you today that you shall surely perish;

you shall not prolong your days in the land which you cross over the Jordan to go in and possess. 19 I call heaven and earth as witnesses today against you, that I have set before you life and death, blessing and cursing; therefore choose life, that both you and your descendants may live; 20 that you may love the Lord your God, that you may obey His voice, and that you may cling to Him, for He is your life and the length of your days; and that you may dwell in the land which the Lord swore to your fathers, to Abraham, Isaac, and Jacob, to give them."

1 Kings 8:56-"Blessed be the Lord, who has given rest to His people Israel, according to all that He promised. There has not failed one word of all His good promise, which He promised through His servant Moses.

Psalm 91:16 -With long life I will satisfy him, And show him My salvation."

Psalm103:3 -Who forgives all your iniquities, Who heals all your diseases,

Psalm 107:20 -He sent His word and healed them, And delivered them from their destructions.

Psalm 118:17 -I shall not die, but live, And declare the works of the Lord.

Proverbs 4:20-23 -My son, give attention to my words; Incline your ear to my sayings. 21 Do not let them depart from your eyes; Keep them in the midst of your heart; 22 For they are life to those who find them, And health to all their flesh. 23 Keep your heart with all diligence, For out of it spring the issues of life.

Isaiah 41:10 -Fear not, for I am with you; Be not dismayed, for I am your God. I will strengthen you, Yes, I will help you, and I will uphold you with My righteous right hand.

Jeremiah 1:12 -Then the Lord said to me, "You have seen well, for I am ready to perform My word."

Jeremiah 30:17 -"For I will restore health to you And heal you of your wounds, "says the Lord, 'Because they called you an outcast saying: "This is Zion; No one seeks her.""

Joel 3:10 -Beat your plowshares into swords And your pruning hooks into spears; Let the weak say, 'I am strong.'"

Nahum 1:9 -What do you conspire against the Lord? He will make an utter end of it. Affliction will not rise up a second time.

Matthew 8:2-3 -And behold, a leper came and worshiped Him, saying, "Lord, if You are willing, You can make me clean."3 Then Jesus put out His hand and touched him, saying, "I am willing; be cleansed." Immediately his leprosy was cleansed.

Matthew 8:17 -That it might be fulfilled which was spoken by Isaiah the prophet, saying: "He Himself took our infirmities, And bore our sicknesses."

Matthew 18:18-19 -"Assuredly, I say to you, whatever you bind on earth will be bound in heaven, and whatever you loose on earth will be loosed in heaven. 19 "Again I say to you that if two of you agree on earth concerning anything that they ask, it will be done for them by My Father in heaven.

Matthew 21:21 -So Jesus answered and said to them, "Assuredly, I say to you, if you have faith and do not doubt, you will not only do what was done to the fig tree, but also if you say to this mountain, 'Be removed and be cast into the sea,' it will be done.

Mark 11:23-24 -For assuredly, I say to you, whoever says to this mountain, 'Be removed and be cast into the sea,' and does not doubt in his heart, but believes that those things he says will be done, he will have whatever he says. 24 Therefore I say to you, whatever things you ask when you pray, believe that you receive them, and you will have them.

Mark 16:17-18 -And these signs will follow those who believe: In My name they will cast out demons; they will speak with new tongues; 18 they will take up serpents; and if they drink anything deadly, it will by no means hurt them; they will lay hands on the sick, and they will recover."

John 10:10 -The thief does not come except to steal, and to kill, and to destroy. I have come that they may have life, and that they may have it more abundantly.

Romans 4:17-20 - (as it is written, "I have made you a father of many nations") in the presence of Him whom he believed—God, who gives life to the dead and calls those things which do not exist as though they did; 18 who, contrary to hope, in hope believed, so that he became the father of many nations, according to what was spoken, "So shall your descendants be." 19 And not being weak in faith, he did not consider his own body, already dead (since he was about a hundred years old), and the deadness of Sarah's womb. 20 He did not waver at the promise of God through unbelief, but was strengthened in faith, giving glory to God.

Romans 8:11 -But if the Spirit of Him who raised Jesus from the dead dwells in you, He who raised Christ from the dead will also give life to your mortal bodies through His Spirit who dwells in you.

2 Corinthians 10:4-5 -For the weapons of our warfare are not carnal but mighty in God for pulling down strongholds, 5 casting down arguments and every high thing that exalts itself against the knowledge of God, bringing every thought into captivity to the obedience of Christ.

Galatians 3:13-14 -Christ has redeemed us from the curse of the law, having become a curse for us (for it is written, "Cursed is everyone who hangs on a tree"), 14 that the blessing of Abraham might come upon the Gentiles in Christ Jesus, that we might receive the promise of the Spirit through faith.

Ephesians 6:10-17 -Finally, my brethren, be strong in the Lord and in the power of His might. 11 Put on the whole armor of God that you may be able to stand against the wiles of the devil. 12 For we do not wrestle against flesh and blood, but against principalities, against powers, against the rulers of the darkness of this age, against spiritual hosts of wickedness in the heavenly places. 13 Therefore take up the whole armor of God that you may be able to withstand in the evil day, and having done all, to stand. 14 Stand therefore, having girded your waist with truth, having put on the breastplate of righteousness, 15 and having shod your feet with the preparation of the gospel of peace; 16 above all, taking the shield of faith with which you will be able to quench all the fiery darts of the wicked one. 17 And take the helmet of salvation, and the sword of the Spirit, which is the word of God.

Philippians 2:13 -For it is God who works in you both to will and to do for His good pleasure.

Philippians 4:6-7 -Be anxious for nothing, but in everything by prayer and supplication, with thanksgiving, let your requests be made known to God; 7 and the peace of God, which surpasses all understanding, will guard your hearts and minds through Christ Jesus.

2 Timothy 1:7 -For God has not given us a spirit of fear, but of power and of love and of a sound mind.

Hebrews 10:23 -Let us hold fast the confession of our hope without wavering, for He who promised is faithful.

Hebrews 10:35 -Therefore do not cast away your confidence, which has great reward.

Hebrews 11:11 -By faith Sarah herself also received strength to conceive seed, and she bore a child when she was past the age, because she judged Him faithful who had promised.

Hebrews 13:8 -Jesus Christ is the same yesterday, today, and forever.

James 5:14-15 -Is anyone among you sick? Let him call for the elders of the church, and let them pray over him, anointing him with oil in the name of the Lord. 15 And the prayer of faith will save the sick, and the Lord will raise him up. And if he has committed sins, he will be forgiven.

1 Peter 2:24 -Who Himself bore our sins in His own body on the tree, that we, having died to sins, might live for righteousness by whose stripes you were healed.

1 John 3:21-22 -Beloved, if our heart does not condemn us, we have confidence toward God. 22 And whatever we ask we receive from Him, because we keep His commandments and do those things that are pleasing in His sight.

1 John 5:14-15 -Now this is the confidence that we have in Him, that if we ask anything according to His will, He hears us. 15 And if we know that He hears us, whatever we ask, we know that we have the petitions that we have asked of Him.

3 John 1:1-2 -The Elder, To the beloved Gaius, whom I love in truth: 2 Beloved, I pray that you may prosper in all things and be in health, just as your soul prospers.

Revelation 12:11 -And they overcame him by the blood of the Lamb and by the word of their testimony, and they did not love their lives to the death.

God's Word Brings Victory

"AGAINST ALL ODDS"

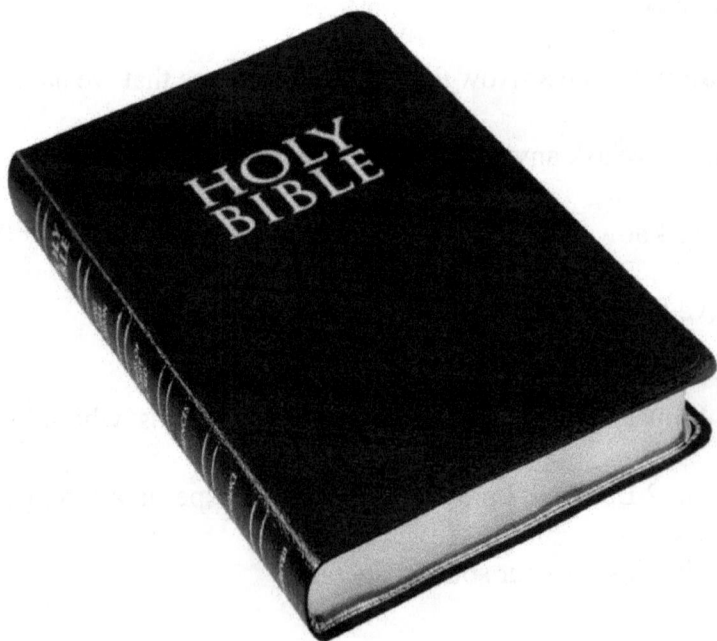

In Loving Memory

To my parents:

Elizabeth Ann Beeler, thank you for being the best mother ever. You sacrificed so much for me. I love you always and forever from my ENTIRE heart.

James O'Neal Smith, thank you daddy for your love and encouraging words on your death bed to return to Jesus Christ. I love you forever.

Mommy and Daddy, I look forward to spending eternity with you both.

To my Grandmother: Ester Smith (Maw Maw)

Thank you for your love, prayers, and always being there for your family. Your encouraging words gave me strength when the odds were against me. You hold a special place in my heart, and in eternity we will never part. A bright shining light you will forever be, beaming in our hearts with every beat. What an angel of love you were to us all, it has kept us together, summer, winter, spring, and fall. Loving you always and forever Maw Maw.

To my First Spiritual Parents Pastor Clifton and First Lady Mollie Russell:

Thank you for cultivating and pruning the seed that was planted and watered in me as a little girl. I am so grateful for the example you were in your ministry and marriage. I am so blessed to be one of the trees that produces fruit from your vineyard. Your fruit shall remain throughout all eternity. I love you both eternally.

To my Aunt Lucille:

Thank you for planting godly seed in me as a little girl. I shall never forget you taking me to Sunday School, choir rehearsals, and Vacation Bible School. I look forward to hearing you sing "He Touched Me and He Made Me Whole" in the heavenly choir.

To my Uncle Leroy Beeler:

Thank you for being a father figure, showing your love and support over the years.

To my Grand-Blessing Serenity:

I miss you so much. You always brought so much joy and peace in my life. I look forward to seeing you in Heaven. You're safe in His arms. Love you always and forever.

To my Brother-In-Love Dax Amir Stewart:

You brought such joy to all of us. Thank you for your love, laughs, and loyalty to your family. Love you always and forever.

To Sis. Geraldine Russell-Ford:

Thank you for watering the seed that was planted in me as a little girl. I shall never forget the teachings in Sunday School that still direct my life today. Forever grateful.

To Sis. Janice Gray:

Thank you for training me up in the youth ministry and imparting the importance of training God's Children. Your legacy lives on.

To Mother Martha Walden:

Thank you for nurturing the gifts of God in me and encouraging me to be all God has called and chosen me to be. I am so grateful for your impartation of preaching and prayer in my life.

To Mrs. Helen Hewlett:

Thank you for your love and support to us and The Faith Church. We are forever grateful for the seeds that you sowed into our ministry.

To Mrs. Dorthella Mathews (Mommy)

Thank you for being such an example and inspiration to me growing up. You brought such a special friend into my life, and I am forever grateful. Your love, support, and prayers made a difference in my life.

Also by this Author

Against All Odds Journal

PREPARING OUR HEARTS FOR HIS WORD IS A WONDERFUL WAY TO START YOUR DAY OF DEVOTION. IT HELPS KEEP YOU FOCUSED AND OPENS UP YOUR HEART TO EMBRACE GOD'S WORD.

PASTOR LAUREN DENISE CARPENTER

Against All ODDS

A-Z Scriptural Journal

3 REASONS A CHRISTIAN SHOULD JOURNAL AFTER READING GOD'S WORD

A GREAT WAY TO HELP YOU REMEMBER WHAT YOU READ

A GREAT WAY TO RECALL THE PROMISES OF GOD OVER YOUR LIFE

A GREAT WAY TO TRACK YOUR ANSWERED PRAYER THROUGH GOD'S WORD

AS I EXPERIENCED THE ODDS AGAINST ME, GOD'S WORD BROUGHT ME VICTORY FROM A-Z

Journal through God's Scriptures from A-Z

Available at:

www.thefaithchurchministries.com

www.amazon.com

www.barnesandnoble.com

www.ingramcontent.com/pod-product-compliance
Lightning Source LLC
Chambersburg PA
CBHW072152090426
42740CB00012B/2230